The Neighbor's Kid

A Cross-Country Journey in Search of What Education Means to Americans

Philip Brand

CAPITAL RESEARCH CENTER

Cover design, typsetting and layout by G. P. Begelman, Inc.

Printed by Excelsior Graphics, New York City

Cover photograph from Veer

Distribution and Sales by AmP Publishers Group
www.amppubgroup.com
(800) 621-8476

LIBRARY OF CONGRESS CATALOGING-IN-PUBLICATION DATA

Brand, Philip, 1985-

The neighbor's kid : a cross-country journey in search of what education means to Americans / Philip Brand.

    p. cm.

Includes bibliographical references and index.

Summary: "Surveys American elementary and secondary education and reports
conversations with teachers, parents and students in forty-nine states"—Provided by publisher.

1. Schools—United States. 2. Education—United States—Public opinion.
3. Public opinion—United States. 4. Educational surveys—United States.
5. Brand, Philip—Travel—United States. I. Title.

LA217.2.B755 2010

370.973—dc22

2010012046

ISBN 978-1-892934-15-4 (pbk.)

To Mom and Dad

About the Author

Philip Brand is the former director of Capital Research Center's Education Watch project. He lives and works in New Hampshire.

Acknowledgements

Every book is based on a few ideas. The idea for the project that became this book took shape while I was researching education issues at the Capital Research Center (CRC). I believed that what I wanted to say about education aligned with the Capital Research Center's mission to promote a robust civil society—the voluntary action and community-based problem solving that Alexis de Tocqueville recognized as a defining feature of our country. I presented my idea of visiting schools across the country to CRC president Terrence Scanlon, who was generous enough to support it. Thank you Terry and the Capital Research Center for making this book possible.

Countless people deserve thanks, beginning with the scores of people who opened the doors of their schools to me. Many of you are included in the book, but some are not. Thank you all. A special thanks goes to my brother Peter, who drew the map of my journey and the illustrations that begin each chapter. I also want to acknowledge two individuals in particular.

Bob Huberty is the first. After every school visit during my nine-month trip I emailed my report to Bob at CRC's offices in Washington, D.C. Through his masterful editing he guided and encouraged me through the duration of the project. His keen insights are reflected on every page. All errors in judgment and fact are of my own making.

My brother Evan is the second person I want to thank, for he agreed to accompany me on this trip. It is an understatement to say that this project would not have happened without his assistance in myriad ways. There is nothing like a good companion on a long journey.

Travels

Legend

- – Chapter 1
- × Chapter 2
- ○ Chapter 3
- △ Chapter 4
- = Chapter 5
- ★ Chapter 6
- ■ Chapter 7

Contents

Chapter 6

Swinging Through the Sunshine States 120

February 26—April 1

Chapter 7

Homeward Bound: Pride and Provincialism 146

April 2—May 13

* = A school discussion out of chronological sequence for thematic reasons.

Topical Index

School consolidation; State remedies for funding disparities

School busing

Single gender schools

Student testing (No Child Left Behind)

School choice through choice of residence

Special Needs and Gifted Education

Sports and Music

Vouchers/Tax Credits

Work-Study/Vocational Education

Introduction

It was going to be a hot July day. But it was still cool and refreshing in the early morning in the foothills of the Catskill Mountains. I was thirteen years old, and my father and I were on a nine-hole golf course only a short walk through the woods from my family's home in upstate New York.

I was playing poorly and had only just reached the tee of the seventh hole, the hardest on the course. It was a mammoth par five, straight up the mountain, with two steep banks breaking the fairway into three tiers and a looming oak tree straight ahead hiding the flag from view. With low expectations I wound up and smacked a drive up the middle. My shot went over the first bank, settling directly before the oak. Confidence boosted, I opted to go over the obstacle. Smack! The ball clacked off the branches. "Try another one," my dad encouraged, so I dropped and hit another ball. And a third and fourth, all into that damned tree. Frustrated at my failure, I let the 5-wood fall to the ground. "These clubs are no good," I mumbled.

My dad's response had a lasting impact on me. Disappointed by my defeatism, he picked up the club, dropped a ball and knocked it high over the tree. "It's not the golf clubs, Phil," he said sternly. The memory is sharp in my mind as is the lesson he imparted.

My dad was teaching me how to distinguish reasons from excuses. He was giving me an education. That's why I begin a book about education with this story. "A proper education," Wendell Berry writes, "enables young people to put their lives in order, which means knowing what things are more important than other things; it means putting first things first." It means learning that it's not the golf clubs' fault.

Berry is right. The rub is that people often disagree on what are the right reasons. For an education off the golf course the goal and the rules are much less clear. Who should decide where kids go to school, what they are taught, and who should pay the cost of their education? In the following pages I will discuss some of the public policy issues raised by these concerns. My focus, however, is on the "felt experience" of the hundreds of students, parents, teachers and administrators I met during my travels. For them education is a daily practice, not a policy issue.

A word about my title, "The Neighbor's Kid." It is meant to convey two central lessons I learned on this trip. The first: When it comes to picking a school many parents care most about the kids with whom their

1

own children associate. Not the curriculum, not the teachers, but the other kids. Sometimes this creates controversy, as in battles over busing, but many parents told me directly that the neighborhood and its children were the principal reason why they chose a school. It was what they thought mattered most in providing the best education for their child.

That brings me to my second conclusion. The more schools I visited the more I became convinced that what happens outside of school—in the home and the community—shapes what happens inside the school. Schools reflect all the kids of all the neighbors. We may not like it, but if we face this reality squarely it will help us understand why education looks as it does in America, and perhaps we will learn what has to be done to improve it.

A Journey

Over the past year I traveled cross-country to 49 states (sorry, Alaska), visiting two schools in each state, to learn more about education in America. As a greenhorn who lacked the years of life-experience that accumulate into something akin to judgment, I found it difficult to think about elementary and secondary education in the abstract. I needed the direct experience of people and places to achieve an understanding in the same way that I needed to be on the golf course to understand my father's lesson in determination.

To keep costs down, I acquired a Volkswagen station wagon whose odometer read 130,000 miles. It ran well enough and on occasion doubled as a nightly refuge with the rear seats down. My brother Evan was my co-pilot. We loaded down the vehicle with a tent and sleeping bags, a camp stove, a basketball, the complete works of Shakespeare (which we never touched), a guitar and harmonica, and what turned out to be a burdensome amount of clothing. On September 3, 2008 we pulled away from our folks' driveway in southern New Hampshire for what was the start of a seven-month road trip.

I wanted to understand American schooling and so I went in search of it. After doing the research, making inquiries and consulting guidebooks and maps I managed to visit nearly one hundred public and private schools, large and small, typical and exceptional. I picked schools in rural, suburban and inner city areas. I visited some schools that represented a traditional model of education—neighborhood public schools that enroll kids whose parents live nearby and pay local property taxes. I also visited with parents who wanted more control of their children's education and so opted out of the system: They enrolled their kids in an independent private school or homeschooled them. And I

2

explored forms of schooling that differ from the traditional neighborhood model—magnet schools, schools created by busing programs, open-enrollment school districts, charter schools, and schools funded by voucher programs.

Any account of schooling in America is necessarily an account of the culture and economy of the country. I stayed with Amish-Mennonites in Lancaster, Pennsylvania and toured their apple farm. I spent Mardi Gras in Mobile, Alabama, and Halloween on an Indian reservation in South Dakota. I was in Manhattan on September 11. I went to honky-tonk bars in rural Mississippi and basketball games in Newark, New Jersey.

For this reason I don't rank schools in any systematic way, nor propose a formula to "fix" education. I am convinced that centralized solutions to education's woes will not work because they cannot address the diverse and local character of education. Worse, centralized solutions corrode the function of families and communities, whose vitality is truly important to a child's education. Look only at schools and we won't see the real issues; broaden our gaze and we might.

* * *

The names of schools and school leaders are accurately identified in the book. The names of teachers, students, parents, friends and community members have been changed.

CHAPTER ONE

Back to School: Fall in New England
September 3 – September 22

Chicken slaughter at the farm school

I pulled out of the driveway of my parents' home on a crisp September morning en route to visit the first school on this tour. My plan was to visit 100 schools in 50 states. This was an adventure, and it was beginning with a combination of anticipation and anxiety mounting to excitement. I'm off! I suspect I'm ill-suited to write on education: I've gone through enough education as a student to think I know it, but haven't been around long enough to have experienced much of the real thing. It's a perfect storm of confidence and ignorance. Well, here goes.

Let me summarize my school visits in September. First stop: St. Johnsbury Academy in Vermont. Its campus of sprawling lawns and white steeples set in a small town atop a rolling hill is picture-perfect New England. St. Johnsbury is a private school, but it's also a local public school, an example of a blurring of the line between public and private schooling that I will see more times than I had supposed. From St. Johnsbury I went on to Vermont's Mountain School, a private high school program where the students make apple cider and slaughter chickens as part of the education curriculum. Vermont is admittedly an atypical state from which to begin a tour of education in America. But it offers a sampling of some of the alternatives to traditional schooling that I'm in search of.

My visit to two New York City public schools, one a charter school, the other a district school, was a striking contrast to my travel through rural Vermont. In Vermont I had only to park my car in a field next to school; in New York City I circled city blocks for an hour to find a coveted spot. I was exasperated even before my day began—a signal for what faces many students and teachers in complex and confusing urban settings.

Before reaching New York City I stopped to visit my grandmother, a former English teacher and writer, and to drop by Roxbury Central School, my old middle school in upstate New York. Roxbury is a small school, and it offers all the opportunities and limitations of its size. My visit sparked a chat about the trade-offs between big and small schools, local control and centralized control.

The traditional public high school that my parents attended in the northwest corner of New Jersey was on my itinerary as was an Albany, New York, single-sex public charter elementary school, the first in the country. And then it was on to Ohio—scheduling glitches sometimes led me to skip over entire states—where I visited a Catholic high school in Cleveland that benefits from the city's school voucher program. I also spent a day at a teacher workshop for a public charter school in Dayton. At the end of three weeks on the road, I was in the Indiana high school gymnasium of basketball legend Larry Bird talking about high school sports, community control, and school vouchers.

September 4, 2008
Antrim, NH

On I-89 the leaves on most trees haven't begun to turn gold. Only patches of fall foliage show themselves in the low wet areas and on the occasional tree turned early. I left my parents' home in Antrim and drove through the middle of New Hampshire, heading north and west. The highway entered the foothills of the White Mountains, through Lebanon, across the Connecticut River, and into Vermont and her rounded Green Mountains.

My brother Evan and I reach bustling Montpelier, capital of Vermont, population 7,500. Further up the road is the small resort town of Stowe. It's off-season for visitors there, and slower and emptier than usual; the tourists who will soon flock to see mountains blanketed in fall colors have not yet arrived.

Stowe specializes in selling the "Vermont brand" and it's what non-Vermonters imagine about the entire state. Bed-and-breakfasts line the street. Nestled among them are stores selling homemade maple syrup products, apple cider and Vermont cheese. We spent the night at the home of our old friends Tom and Joanna where even the dog loved cheese. Welcome to Vermont. The Ben and Jerry's ice cream factory is here, and the Vermont Teddy Bear Company. Stowe, one of Vermont's larger northern towns, is quiet this time of year, underscoring the state's rural character.

We left Stowe and drove around and over soft hills to reach the town of St. Johnsbury whose Academy I was scheduled to visit at 8:00 a.m. the next day. Two miles outside town we pitched our tent at a local RV campground. The campground was a small cul-de-sac adorned with fluorescent pink palm trees and lined with fifty RVs, many of them seemingly fixed in place. Some sported porches, gardens and satellite dishes. Elderly people sat at picnic tables and poked at their campfires. I found the scene so disorienting that upon first entering the campground I drove around the circle and headed out. How bizarre. The RV campground was a little circle of modern-day teepees for a tribe of travelers.

I felt a bit nervous setting up camp and began to worry that my first school visit would be a flop, somehow disproving the concept of the project. The last time I wandered along hallways teeming with a thousand high school students I was one of them. Evan and I started a campfire and began cooking noodles on our camp stove. It was dark and we forgot to bring a lamp or cutlery. Up to my wrists in pasta, I gave up and retired to my sleeping bag.

September 5, 2008
St. Johnsbury Academy, St. Johnsbury Vermont

I began my day as the students who are here begin every day. At eight we attended Chapel, or what some schools call morning meeting. A hush fell over the students and staff as the headmaster took the stage. "In Asian cultures," he began, "to know someone's name is to know a person intimately." His message was about the importance of community at St. Johnsbury. Students, teachers, custodians, everyone should know one another's names. He challenged the senior class to learn the names of every senior, offering $100 to any student who could do it.

The emphasis on school community makes sense because a town like St. Johnsbury—everyone calls it St J.—also has a strong sense of community. Browsing through the local paper on the day of my visit, I found this in the police log: "A tripod was found in the area of Pleasant and Church streets. The owner may claim it at the police department with proper identification."

But there's another reason to emphasize community. Because it is both a local school and a boarding school, St. J Academy has a diverse student body. Three-quarters of its 1000 students are day students from the town and surrounding area, but 250 are boarders who come from across the country and overseas, particularly from Asia. The boarding students are plunked down in a small town in the least racially diverse part of the least diverse state in the nation. It's a big cultural adjustment for both the boarding students and the locals. The director of the boarding school told me he was dealing with one boy from Kazakhstan who was wretched with homesickness.

Besides the cultural divide, there is a wealth divide. Local day students attend the school free of charge, while boarding students pay upwards of $40,000 for tuition, room and board. Billionaires' kids and kids who are growing up in trailer parks—the St. J. area is one of the poorest in Vermont—go to class side by side. To blunt the social divide the school requires all students to take turns as waiters and dishwashers during mealtimes.

I met with headmaster Tom Lovett, a middle-aged man with a master's degree in English literature. His grizzled beard and lean features give him a weathered look. Lovett explains the reasons for the unusual arrangement of a private school that also serves as the town's public school. The system is called "town tuitioning," and it's unique to rural areas in New England.

Vermont is a rural state—it has slightly more than half as many *residents* as the New York City school district has *students*—and the state's education system is shaped by its rural character. When Vermont drafted its first constitution on July 4, 1777, it mandated that all towns provide public schools. But with fiercely independent local communities spread out across a rugged terrain, the provision was difficult to maintain. Less than ten years later the state constitution was changed to say that towns "ought" to maintain schools to provide children with an education.

Vermont towns, proud of their self-reliance, fulfilled their constitutional responsibility by constructing private academies. These schools developed a reputation for providing quality education, and Vermonters grew attached to them.

Enter Horace Mann, Secretary to the newly-created Massachusetts' Board of Education. During the second quarter of the nineteenth century he took scattered local schools and created a common school system in Massachusetts. Through his writings and speeches he popularized the idea of centralizing control over public primary and secondary education, creating the Massachusetts model that most states would follow.

Concerned that the new system in Massachusetts infringed on local control, Vermont hesitated to adopt it. As one Vermonter would write, "Widespread respect for private academies and acknowledgement of the impracticality of each town's building its own school" led Vermont to come up with an alternative to Horace Mann's model. In 1869 Vermont passed the state's first "tuitioning" statute: Rather than require that each town build its own school, the law allowed towns without a school to pay for their students to attend a private academy in an adjoining district. The new law "essentially made the creation of public schools in every district unnecessary." This statute was soon expanded so that students could use the money provided by the town and state government to attend schools outside the neighboring district and even outside the state.

With this system, Vermonters publicly provided for the education of every child, while also maintaining the tradition of town academies. Today private schools in Vermont that accept publicly funded students must be non-religious, have state approval, and abide by Vermont education laws. It's hard to believe, but even today one in three Vermont towns has no public school and continues to use this tuition voucher system. To enable their students to attend public or private schools, the so-called "tuition towns" share education expenses with the state of Vermont. Together, they provide the tuition vouchers that are equivalent to the approximate cost of educating a child in a Vermont public school.

St. J. is a tuition town. In the 1870s, the town of St. Johnsbury decided to convert its high school into a grade school and to use voucher money to send its high school students to the private St. J. Academy, which was cheaper. The headmaster told me that St. J's attractive facilities—it really looks like a miniature college campus—and its reputation for excellence have created a public perception that the school is for the elite. Lovett said this was untrue: "We accept every kid who applies here." But as in other communities with good schools, some high-achieving Vermont parents move to the St. J. area for the school, causing a "brain-drain" at other schools.

As a private school that accepts no federal funding, St. J. Academy doesn't have to comply with the federal No Child Left Behind (NCLB) Act, the 2002 law that sets national standards for student achievement. From Headmaster Lovett's perspective, that's a good thing. He believes Washington, D.C. isn't the place to craft policies for St. J. But the school is implementing a new program called Schools Attuned, which has goals similar to NCLB. A teacher I spoke with explained that St. J. Academy doesn't disagree with NCLB's goals, "We just think we have a better model for achieving them."

Evan and I ate lunch in the school cafeteria (chicken patty, fries and chocolate milk). Except for mandatory ties on the boys and conservative outfits for the girls, St. J students looked like most other high school students pushing through a lunch line and jostling about the cafeteria. Over lunch I asked a guidance counselor to name her biggest challenge. Her predictable answer: Overanxious parents. They want their kids to attend a "top" college for its "wow" factor. She said it's a constant struggle to convince students and parents that their goal should be to find the "right" college that fits the student's academic needs.

September 8, 2008
The Mountain School, Vershire, Vermont

The man said he could "do" 35 an hour—slaughter chickens, that is.

You can conjure up an image of a chicken slaughter, but the reality is faster and less messy. Behind the dining hall and kitchen of the Mountain School there is a parked pickup truck with a white trailer attached. It's a portable slaughtering shop, and the man had been doing it for thirteen years. Next to the trailer are crates of broiler chickens that have been raised on the school grounds. The animals are docile, clucking or rustling about only occasionally.

The butcher grabs the first chicken by its legs, puts it upside down into a stainless steel cone, so the chicken's head sticks out the small end at the bottom. Beneath the cone is a trash can, which catches the blood after the butcher slices the chicken's throat with a knife. He does a second, and a third and a fourth, each in its own cone. By the time the fourth chicken is killed, the first chicken has stopped flailing about with involuntary nerve convulsions. The butcher told us the bird dies the instant its throat is cut.

The four chickens are then plopped into boiling water as the butcher starts slaughtering a new batch. When the second batch has been killed, he takes the first batch out of the boiler, one at a time, and holds them up against a spinning brush, which in no time removes the feathers. It's a three-step process—decapitate, boil, pluck—taking no more than a couple of minutes per bird.

I stood there with the Mountain School students and watched. One girl threw up and cried. It's a serious job, and I was surprised at how efficiently the man went about his work.

Though a chicken slaughter is not an everyday affair, it represents what's at the heart and soul of the Mountain School, which is dedicated to connecting students to the process and context of everyday affairs: Do you want to know where food comes from? How it's grown? What's in the forests that surround the school? How do you create a sense of community? What's to be learned in rural Vermont? It's why all Mountain School students are encouraged to walk to the back of the school and witness the chicken slaughter.

The Mountain School is near Vershire, a town that consists of a couple buildings clustered near the road surrounded by fields full of giant piles of firewood and hay bales wrapped in white plastic to look like big pieces of Chiclet gum. The school program is only a semester long: Twice a year for four months in the spring and fall forty to fifty juniors and seniors from high schools across America work on an organic farm while attending a regular schedule of classes. Work activities vary by season: Students plant and harvest a three-acre vegetable garden, fence in pasture for cows and sheep, make apple cider, and care for the turkeys and chickens that will feed the school the following year.

Breakfast was my first school activity. Learning to prepare food and eat it is something the school takes seriously. Kids go through the food line and take seats at the nearest table in a circular room, filling up each table before occupying the next. No one sits alone and eating partners change daily. A chart on the wall prominently lists the students' chores: help prepare food, feed the pigs, clean the bathrooms.

The Mountain School advertises itself as "a place of intellectual

10

energy, stunning beauty, spontaneous play, and unrelenting honesty." But the kids tell me the biggest difference from their regular schools is the student body. Everyone is here by choice. It takes a certain kind of young person to leave high school for a semester to live on a working farm in the middle of Vermont, with internet access limited to the library and no cell phones. The only way to catch Red Sox games is on the radio.

Typical days run from 8:00 in the morning to 6:30 in the evening, including a three hour work period in the afternoon. I sat in on U.S. History, where John, a young teacher in his fourth year at the Mountain School, gathered a dozen engaged students around a big square table. The class text was Eric Foner's *Give Me Liberty!*, a book recommended for first year college students. In a class in environmental science I tramped through the woods to learn about forest disturbances. The teacher said half of the school's classes are held outdoors, which lifts the kids' spirits and encourages them to reflect on what they see and hear. I am reminded of a term—"nature-deficit disorder"—coined by author Richard Louv in his book *Last Child in the Woods*. Louv argues that when young people are kept indoors they are prone to obesity, attention disorders and depression. Instead of talking about environmentalism, Louv says kids need to walk in the woods. He writes:

"When I was a kid I had an intimate knowledge of woods and fields…I really had a sense of ownership—I had no clue that my woods were connected to other woods ecologically. It's the reverse now. Kids today can tell you lots of things about the Amazon rain forest; they can't usually tell you the last time they lay out in the woods and watched the leaves move…the problem is, it becomes an intellectualized relationship with nature. And I don't think there's much that can replace wet feet and dirty hands. It's one thing to read about a frog, it's another to hold it in your hand and feel its life."

A three-hour work assignment follows lunch (homegrown lamb, beef and greens), and for my group that means apple-picking and apple-sorting, one pile for cider, one for sauce. Others students cut and split wood. It is a mix of work and talk and play.

With its focus on chicken slaughter and apple-picking, and classes held outdoors or seated around a square table, the Mountain School program is strikingly at odds with most school programs that are designed to prepare students for a modern life. The school's old-fashioned focus on rural life and its emphasis on daily routine mirror the ideas of Wendell Berry, a farmer and writer. In a 1989 commencement address to students at the College of the Atlantic in Bar Harbor,

Maine, Berry offered this advice: "Understand that no amount of education can overcome the innate limits of human intelligence and responsibility. We are not smart enough or conscious enough or alert enough to work responsibly on a gigantic scale."

September 9, 2008
Roxbury Central School, Roxbury, New York

It's a three-minute walk from my grandmother's apartment to Roxbury Central School (RCS), the middle school I attended in seventh and eighth grades before my family moved to New Hampshire. Roxbury is a quiet town in the foothills of the Catskill Mountains, the place where, as Washington Irving tells it, Rip Van Winkle fell asleep and woke up twenty years later. It's only a little less sleepy now, having become a place of second homes for folks from New York City. I hadn't been back to my old school since I left, but my science teacher greeted me as soon as I walked through the door. When I was a student he seemed older; now he seems younger than when I last saw him a dozen years ago. As we chatted about the cars and rockets I built for class projects I noticed a wall chart going back twenty years and listing the names of all the members of the school's science teams. There was my name: bronze medal, regional egg-drop competition. In a small school everyone really does know your name.

While waiting for a meeting with Tom, the district superintendent and a former RCS principal, I watched kids of all ages shuffle in and out of the main office. RCS houses students from preschool and kindergarten through 12th grade in one building, a practice that's not uncommon in this area. But even with 14 grades the school has just over 300 students. Tom said mixing five year olds with 17-year olds in the same school building is no problem for a small school. Younger students are neither overwhelmed nor overrun—"They're used to it, it's all most of them have known."

We talked about teachers unions, and student drug and alcohol use, and my old classmates and teachers. Eventually our conversation got around to testing. Tom, who once taught social studies, argued that the No Child Left Behind law mandating standardized testing is an infringement on the states' rights. "I know that when the Founding Fathers wrote the Constitution they gave the states the right to educate, not the federal government."

I also talked with the school psychologist, who said a small school like Roxbury gives students opportunities. He recalled how an "unpopular" girl was beaming when the softball team needed an extra player and invited her to join it. At RCS, a student rarely gets cut from anything. Of course in other ways small size means less opportunity: the choice of classes and range of extracurricular activities is more limited. But there are real benefits in a small school like Roxbury, particularly the pride and sense of ownership that spurs school involvement and responsibility. During my visit I watched my cousin's wife chaperone their three young children around school. I recognized former teachers who join the golf tournament I play in every summer. They are part of the community and the community is part of the school. When Evan and I ate dinner with our extended family later that night, there were former and current RCS students, a former school board member, a town councilman and a teacher seated around the table.

September 11, 2008
New Heights Academy Charter School,
New York City, New York

It takes three hours to drive from Roxbury to New York City where I visited New Heights Academy Charter School located at 150th Street and Amsterdam Avenue, in Washington Heights, just north of Harlem. What I thought was a smart decision to take a bus to the school turned out to be a mistake when I caught a local uptown bus that stopped about every four feet for commuter traffic and swarms of school children. I arrived disheveled and an hour late.

New Heights is a charter school, which means it is publicly funded but not operated by the local school district. As a charter school it doesn't have to abide by many of the regulations imposed on traditional public schools. But to maintain its taxpayer funding it must be accountable for its students' achievement and reach levels specified in the school's charter of incorporation. New Heights received its charter in 2005, and it is set to enroll middle and high school students at all grade levels next year. Enrollment reflects the area's demographic breakdown: 80 percent Latino and 20 percent black. Almost every student qualifies for a free or reduced-price lunch.

Principal Stacy Winitt is young and energetic, talks quickly and cuts to the chase. She said many of her nearly 400 students struggled at traditional public schools and arrive at New Heights years behind in academic grade level. She said it's true that the families of charter school kids are more involved in their child's education than other parents, but that this didn't mean traditional public schools were losing the smarter or better-behaved kids to charter schools. "Often parents are involved because their kids are having trouble in school. They are the ones frustrated with the current system, and they come to us."

13

As an independent public school, New Heights can experiment with different policies. It has fewer class periods, but they last longer. The school day is longer too, so teachers receive ten percent more pay than other city public school teachers. There is a twenty-four student cap on class size, "which is unheard of in New York City public high schools." Students wear uniforms, and the students I spoke with were surprisingly supportive of the policy. With uniforms "we avoid a lot of problems," one boy said. "I have more clothes for the weekend." "I'm used to it," a tenth grade girl chimed in, "and now I don't have to stand in front of the mirror all morning."

Even as it provides a longer school day and smaller class size, New Heights doesn't receive as much taxpayer money per pupil as a traditional public school. How does the school do it? Winitt explained that the school saves money by having fewer administrative staff positions: "We aren't top-heavy."

Winitt is an alumnus of the Teach for America (TFA) program, which recruits bright college graduates who want to teach but did not major in education or receive an education credential. "I love TFA," she said, "and many of my teachers are TFA. They just bring an energy that is essential." A woman in her second year in TFA taught the class I visited. She had her students line up outside the door before class, and she greeted all of them by name, shaking their hands as they entered: "Now give me a firm shake, and look me in the eye." Many students, she said, don't know how to interact with adults in a professional and courteous manner. "Listen to me with your eyes and ears," she said as she roamed about the room, always on the move, gesturing with her arms and body, patting a kid on the back or peeking over a girl's shoulder.

The energy of new teachers complements the wisdom of the more experienced teachers. "I couldn't imagine having all new teachers," the principal said, and I think her young teachers would agree; a mentor is crucial during the first several years. But age is probably a less important factor than "fit." Teachers need to fit the grade level they teach, and the culture of the school. "I switched a teacher from middle school to high school, and the results were amazing," Winnit said. And while there's a camaraderie between teachers at New Heights, the charter school culture of high expectations and increased public visibility is a demanding one. It's not for everyone.

Winnit has asked several teachers not to come back. She has the freedom to do that because everyone hired at New Heights is an at-will employee. Winnit said it takes years to fire a bad teacher in a typical New York City public school, and that just wouldn't cut it at New Heights. "That's a lot of kids' educations squandered." Most of all, Winnit says the culture of teaching needs to change. "There is a tenure mindset, an entitlement mindset. I'm not anti-union, I'm anti-bad union."

Sitting in one of those uncomfortable combination chair-desk contraptions, I chatted with three New Heights' students in a tiled hallway. Two Hispanic girls and a boy, they overcame their nervous fidgetiness and quietly made an argument for their school that is more compelling than any amount of data or expert opinion: They said at New Heights there are fewer fights. "Why is that?" I asked. The boy pondered the question for a moment and then replied, "There aren't as many kids here who get in fights." Of course! Fewer kids who are likely to get in fights means a safer school for everyone else. One of the girls chimed in that the school's smaller size had something to do with it. "My old school was so big I didn't know anyone, and I ain't never met the principal. Ms. Winnit, she's everywhere."

September 12, 2008
C.S. 211, New York City, New York

I visited C.S. 211 on Friday, September 12, one day after the seventh anniversary of 9/11. Twin white lights now shine brightly into the night sky to commemorate where the towers once stood in lower Manhattan, but the anniversary seemed to pass in the Bronx without much sense of occasion. In a seventh grade classroom the teacher asked his students, "What makes someone a hero?" The bulletin board was covered with responses written on pink Post-it notes:

"The word hero means to me is somebody who helps you if you get hurt has your back all the time."

"The word hero mean that a person protects us and protects poor people."

"A hero means to me doing something great in the world. Like those firefighters on 9/11 or saving the world, or like Jesus Christ on the cross so we can live."

C.S. 211 is a pre-k through eighth grade New York City public school (C.S. stands for Community School). The school neighborhood which clusters around a subway stop—East Tremont Avenue—is homogenous. It's almost all Hispanic, mostly Dominican. Luke, the teacher who hosted my day's visit, told me the area's ethnicity is so uniform that many of his kids don't realize they are a minority in the United States. The few non-Hispanics I encountered at the subway were all teachers. A young woman who got off the train two stops before me carried a bag that said

15

Bronx Charter School. Another young woman at my stop was just out of college. She asked if I was a teacher. I told her I was visiting C.S. 211, which turned out to be where she taught. We walked together to school.

English is the second language in the neighborhood around C.S. 211, and many of the school's students are classified as English Language Learners (ELLs). C.S. 211 is a bilingual school, so some courses are taught in Spanish. I observed that some of the school's staff had a limited command of English.

Luke teaches seventh grade math. Since he has 35 students in each class—common in this school—maintaining order is a prerequisite for learning. Luke talks and walks about the classroom as his kids play "Buzz," a counting game meant to help them learn the multiplication tables. They are on the edge of their seats playing the game, which is intended to develop skills in listening and teamwork as well as math. The students were eager to teach me the rhythmic clapping routine that's part of the game.

While Luke's classroom was well under control, another classroom I visited grew chaotic as soon as the bell rang and stayed that way during most of the class period. Many students wandered in and out of the class or sat talking to one another. They showed little respect for their teacher and tuned her out whenever she yelled at them. Later when I was trying to meet up with Luke at lunch he was approached by a girl screaming that a boy had groped her in the hall. "Go on, man, I've got to deal with this," he said as he corralled the students to sort out the issue. So much for Luke's lunch break.

What explains breakdowns in discipline? Certainly good teachers have rough days, and sometimes kids are just determined to bounce off the walls. Nonetheless, I couldn't help but think that part of the problem with the unruly class was the teacher, who gave out an assignment mainly intended to use up class time. She asked her art class students to "draw lines" for the entire period, which was bound to produce restlessness. I don't know what the assignment was meant to teach, but her effort to stifle boisterous students was sure to backfire. Kids may groan when they are required to address hard problems, but it's a lot easier to keep them engaged when they have to learn something that's difficult and challenging.

Luke said it isn't easy to work in a school like C.S. 211. What's needed, he said, isn't more resources, but teachers who are both empowered and held accountable. Luke said the teachers' union is "terrible" about that. "At this school, we have really good teachers and really poor teachers." I question how C.S. 211 can empower its teachers and hold them accountable if New York City schools and teacher unions won't acknowledge that there are big differences in teacher quality.

Some weeks later Luke told me that he was leaving C.S. 211 at the end of the year. He was going to a charter school where the teachers were more motivated to take charge of their classes.

September 15, 2008
Newton High School, Newton, New Jersey

The town of Newton and its public high school are set in the middle of Sussex County in northwest New Jersey, and they don't fit the state's stereotype. Newton is not on the turnpike and it doesn't contain huge factories and sprawling warehouses. Instead, the town is situated among rolling hills where horses graze and farm stands sell corn and tomatoes. Places like Newton earned the state its "Garden State" nickname. My visit to Newton High School (NHS) began with a tour of the school's greenhouses and fish tanks, facilities in its excellent agriculture program. The program also provides its students with training and equipment to hang, dress, and store a deer.

My parents are graduates of NHS ('72 and '76) and it was fun to look at their old yearbooks, which reflect the styles of another time. But while a group photo of "Future Homemakers"—all women—is unlikely to find a place in today's yearbook, my impression of NHS was one of continuity, not change. Apart from the conspicuous difference in hairstyles (why so much hair back then?), NHS today was not dissimilar from NHS in the 1970s, and my parents' high school memories seemed not so different from the experiences recounted by the NHS students I met. Newton students told me some of their teachers and classes were good and some were poor, but what concerned them most was what one Newton student called the "normal drama of high school." The students enjoy an "open campus" at lunchtime. "We get to go outside off campus for lunch, go outside to smoke. That's the best part about this school," one boy told me.

Allowing for these dismissive "too cool for school" attitudes, NHS appeared to be a fine place for a teenager to spend four years. I met principal Jim Tasker, who eagerly jumped into a discussion about high stakes education testing. "As a chemistry professor, I know nature detests perfection; it likes diversity," he said. Tasker scoffed at the No Child Left Behind (NCLB) law, which requires the states to measure student achievement and implausibly mandates that schools ensure that all students reach reading and math standards of "proficiency" or face sanctions, Tasker said, "If the federal government wants perfection, why don't they mandate it for themselves." He questioned whether proficiency in educational achievement can be achieved school-wide and noted, "As my father always used to tell me, the world needs ditch diggers too."

Tasker distrusts politicians—"Politicians don't care about kids, the only reason they care about education is because of the money"—and it was clear that his view of NCLB stemmed at least in part from his state's climate of corruption. If "Trenton is a political garbage dump," then it's understandable that you don't want it to run the schools. The state, said Tasker, has "taken away too much local control in a variety of areas. I don't mind state tests. We'll meet them, but don't tell us how to meet them. Don't set our curriculum." He said school district leaders should be treated like adults, not children: "Give us flexibility, and sure we'll make some mistakes, but on the whole we will do a better job than the state," he said.

Tasker thinks more state and federal oversight isn't the answer. But he is skeptical of school vouchers and doubts they can dramatically improve school achievement. "You can bring in all the vouchers you want, but you won't get much improvement when we spend our time teaching kids about drugs, sex and character education." Character education is better done at home and in church, he said. Tasker argued that culture is upstream from education. For there to be educational improvements at school there must be changes in what's taught at home, and kids need to be in settled households enjoying some measure of economic security. "They expect us to be able to change the culture through the schools. I'm not sure that's possible. Whose character are we teaching anyway?"

September 16, 2008
Brighter Choice Charter School for Boys, Albany, New York

I had driven through Albany on my way to New York City but back-tracked to visit a charter school that has the distinction of being an innovative school choice site as well as the nation's first single-sex public elementary school.

In 1997 New York City philanthropist Virginia Gilder undertook an experiment. She selected the lowest-performing public elementary school in Albany—Giffen Memorial—and offered to pay 90 percent of the tuition for any Giffen student who wanted to attend a private school. Nearly one fifth of Giffen's students took Gilder up on her offer, including the child of Giffen's PTA president.

18

The project, called A Better Choice (ABC), used private money to help Giffen students attend a better private school. But Gilder's philanthropy had another purpose that put Albany public school officials on the spot. She was asking some tough questions: Why continue funding public schools where children don't learn, and why force low-income parents to send their children to these schools? Why not let government money follow children to schools that their parents choose, including private ones, ones where they can learn?

Gilder's philanthropy had yet another goal. By offering students a choice, she believed the availability of school alternatives would also give Giffen an incentive to improve itself. That's what seems to have happened. To prevent students from abandoning the school, Albany school officials hired new administrators and teachers, bought new books and equipment, and improved teacher training. As a *New York Times* story reported, "In their overhaul of Giffen, city school officials seem to have inadvertently bolstered a central argument for vouchers: that they foster competition and thereby force public schools to improve." *Forbes Magazine* published a cover story about the experiment, reporting that it had prompted the creation of at least ten new private voucher programs.

One other important consequence of Gilder's philanthropy was its impact on the ABC project, whose officers went on to write the law authorizing the creation of charter schools in New York. The acronym now stands for Albany Brighter Choice, which operates two publicly funded charter schools, one for boys and one for girls. On a dreary and overcast mid-September morning I visited the Brighter Choice Charter School for Boys (BCCS), which opened in 2002 as the first single-sex public elementary school in the country. A comparable girls' campus is down the street.

Until recently, there were no single-sex public elementary schools. Title IX of the Education Amendments of 1972 essentially wiped out single sex education. (Title IX is the hotly contested 37-word amendment to the Elementary and Secondary Education Act best known for requiring parity in spending for men's and women's college athletic programs.) But that began to change in 2001 when Senators Kay Bailey Hutchinson (R-TX) and Hillary Clinton (D-NY) teamed up to open the door to single sex public education. In 2006, the U.S. Department of Education rewrote Title IX, giving local districts the option to offer single sex schools and programs. There are currently over 400 public schools across the country providing these options.

As a charter school, ABC enrollment is open to all students, but a preference is given to poor families in the Albany area. The student body is all black and nearly all poor. Darryl Williams, the school's principal, told me his school is a response to an outcry by parents in the community. Chris Bender, executive director of the Brighter Choice Foundation, agreed. He pointed out that approximately one in five Albany city residents pay to send their children to private schools instead of Albany public schools, a disproportionately high number. BCCS was created to provide a charter school option for families with limited means who couldn't afford private tuition. The Brighter Choice Foundation now acts as a support organization for ten charter schools in operation or planned for the Albany area.

I could see the value of an all-boys environment. The boys in a kindergarten class enthusiastically followed their teacher's lead in singing and dancing to a song about a grandma going shopping. Mr. Williams said the school understands the learning style of boys, and plays to their strengths while compensating for their weaknesses. "Boys don't value effort as much as they value results," said Williams, "so we really emphasize the effort side with our students."

Williams said that at the end of the school day between 20 and 40 percent of his students go home to "chaos." But kids can overcome difficult and even desperate conditions, he said, citing his own personal story as the reason for his high expectations. "There's no replacement for a good home environment," he said, but not having one doesn't mean you can't succeed. Williams' mother was murdered when he was two years old and he was raised by a grandmother in the South Bronx. He learned to write by composing letters to his father in prison.

The results Brighter Choice gets are inspiring. Both the boys and girls schools have been ranked as the #1 public elementary school in Albany. Their students routinely outperform Albany district schools in statewide English and math exams.

September 17, 2008
Cleveland Central Catholic School, Cleveland, Ohio

Greetings from Slavic Village. In this ethnic Cleveland neighborhood there are large numbers of residents of Polish and Czech descent, as well as many African Americans. When I arrived in Slavic Village I went to Cleveland Central Catholic High School (CCCS), where I was warmly welcomed by its principal, Sister Allison Marie Gusdanovic.

CCCS is a coeducational Catholic high school with a ballooning enrollment. Sister Gusdanovic said the increase is thanks to the Cleveland Scholarship and Tutoring Program. Passed in 1996, the

Cleveland program provides families of meager means with a government education voucher they can use to help cover tuition costs at area private schools, including religious schools. A sizable majority of Cleveland Central Catholic's students are voucher students.

Sister Gusdanovic told me that families have four reasons for choosing CCCS: academic achievement, concern for culture and discipline, religion, and safety. Cleveland Public Schools face the same issues as schools in many other urban areas, including violence and low academic achievement. In the years before the voucher program was enacted, students in Cleveland Public Schools had an annual 1-in-14 chance of becoming a school crime victim. But CCCS is different. For some students, said Sister Gusdanovic, the school is the only place where they feel safe.

Most but not all of the school staff are Catholic. "I am looking for faith-filled individuals," Sister Gusdanovic told me. The school day begins with a student-read prayer over the PA and each class begins with a prayer. In a science class I watched as the teacher explained: "Prayer is a daily reminder to our minds to live our values." Classes in theology round out the high school curriculum.

While the school is Catholic, the students don't need to be. In fact, because so many students use vouchers to attend school for non-religious reasons, less than half come from Catholic families. Sister Gusdanovic quoted the late James Cardinal Hickey, a former bishop of Cleveland who became archbishop of Washington, DC: "We do it not because they're Catholic, but because we're Catholic."

After science class, I went to lunch, a boisterous affair. Discipline was pervasive in the classroom, but in the cafeteria students released their pent-up energy. I sat with boys who shouted out tales of football practice while gulping chocolate milk. I asked the alpha male of the group to tell me something about his school. He looked across the dimly-lit basement bustling with students and nodded to a table of girls: "Those girls are sexy." At another table I asked a girl the same question: Tell me about your school. She replied with an exuberant, "I'm the best. Write about me!" A barrage of names and calls of, "No, I'm the best," followed.

What makes Catholic schools different? I asked the question to one teacher, a middle-aged man completing his dissertation on the subject. He reached into his bag and handed me his dissertation's thesis page: "To summarize, I contend that there exists in Catholic schools a dynamic of interpersonal relationships and support that is based on the experienced and believed Catholicism of its members, beginning first with the adult staff persons that filters to the students...The adult staff persons have a common understanding of who they are, their deepest mission, and what it means to educate young people."

Yes, it sounded like a dissertation, but it captured what happens at CCCS, a school that has created a coherent and supportive learning environment.

September 19, 2008
Dayton View Academy, Dayton, Ohio

I arrived in Dayton several days after a fierce windstorm swept through southern Ohio. With traffic lights still out every car made a point of stopping at every intersection. Trees were splintered and toppled, and the ground was covered with those grapefruit-sized green nuts that hang from trees in this part of the country.

The students at Dayton View Academy were off most of the week because of the windstorm. Only teachers and staff were at school on the Friday I visited, and the day was devoted to the kind of management training session common to all kinds of office jobs across America. It's called "professional development."

The teachers were laid-back and dressed-down. A group of 40 laughed and bantered comfortably—though the habit of addressing one another as "Mrs. Hathaway" or "Ms. Jane" carried over from when students are present. Like elementary schools around the country, more than 90 percent of the Academy's teachers are women.

The thing that struck me about the school's work environment was its non-hierarchical character. Besides the principal, who led the discussion, all the teachers seemed on the same level. They clustered around tables, sitting in little kid chairs, and worked in teams. One man, his hair in dreadlocks, cracked self-effacing jokes about how math wasn't his specialty. The other teachers in his group laughed and the principal took a friendly jab at him.

Dayton View is a public charter school run by Edison Schools, a for-profit company. Edison is one of largest firms in the industry, but there are others. For-profit management of public schools came on the education scene in the early 1990s, and it has grown in tandem with, and largely thanks to, the growth of charter schools.

In the 1990s, Edison's founder Chris Whittle had big plans for the private operation of schools. His book *Crash Course* imagines the future of schooling. Whittle described what it will be like when global education firms with billions of dollars in revenue run schools around the world.

The bright future of global education that Whittle imagined may be more dream than reality. I think the problem lies with the nature of education, which is necessarily personal and local. Increasing the size and scale of education to save money creates costly trade-offs, and the most costly is parental involvement. Researchers have shown that large, highly centralized school systems are likely to discourage family participation in a child's education. According to Harvard economist Caroline Hoxby, family variables—including such things as whether parents have knowledge of their child's homework assignments and whether they attend parent-teacher conferences—are among the most powerful factors influencing student achievement. Slight improvements in family conduct can improve a child's education more than big increases in other school inputs.

If that is the case, then achieving economies of scale won't improve a child's education. The idea of global education in which decisions are aggregated and out-sourced won't work. Educating children is labor-intensive and one-on-one. It's a fundamentally different enterprise from manufacturing widgets.

September 22, 2008
Springs Valley High School, French Lick, Indiana

We've been on the road for 19 days and are now in French Lick, a small town in southern Indiana that gets its name from the salt deposits on the rocks around the area's mineral springs. Deer and buffalo used to come to the springs to lick the salt off the rocks. In the 1830s the mineral springs began attracting a new crowd: visitors from a hundred miles away arrived to soak up the "miracle waters" of the mineral baths. I'm not sure whether any of them were French.

By the late 1800s, seven rail lines brought guests to the French Lick Springs Hotel and its neighboring West Baden Springs Hotel. The resorts achieved international renown and surrounded themselves with golf courses, gambling casinos, an opera house, and a two-deck pony and bicycle track. Until the 1964 construction of the Houston Astrodome, the West Baden Springs Hotel was home to the country's (and for a time the world's) largest unsupported dome—the birds inside flew between palm trees and there was a massive fireplace that burned 14-foot logs. At least that's what they say in West Baden.

I wasn't aware of this history when I pulled into the parking lot of Springs Valley High School, which serves both French Lick and West Baden Springs. I came for a different history: to see the high school where Larry Bird played basketball. The NBA star would lead the

Boston Celtics to three championships during the 1980's. As I snapped a picture of the school gymnasium, it was clear that the students eating lunch there didn't share my sense of awe. Living in a place normalizes it, while idolatry is best experienced at a distance.

I met the school's athletic director, who was Bird's middle school basketball coach 40 years ago. He told me Bird was only a mediocre player in middle school. "Then he shot up six inches and played basketball nonstop." He smiled fondly and reminisced about the times when the gym used to fill up when Bird played. "We had thousands of people in here for his games; we were way over fire code." Visitors still regularly come to the school from around the country and across the world to see where Bird played ball. Today, the girls' athletic teams are better across the board that the boys', but neither basketball team has been a powerhouse for years.

I played basketball in high school in New Hampshire, where basketball isn't a big deal, and our team was lousy. Even still, it drew together most of the parents and many other members of our town on game nights. The support was energizing, but it pales in comparison to Friday nights in Indiana. They really do resemble the movie "Hoosiers," which was inspired by the true story of Milan High School, a small Indiana high school that won the state basketball championship in 1954.

In Indiana, thousands of locals stuff themselves into gymnasiums to witness long-running rivalries. "This intense loyalty," observed journalist Michael Gerson in 1997, "also serves a more useful purpose, expressing and creating a sense of community." Towns "define their identity through regional basketball rivalries—the opportunity to build community pride by humbling their neighbors."

Indiana's proud attachment to local public schools and their basketball traditions shapes how residents view education reform. Gerson took a tour of small-town Indiana when the state was considering a voucher program in 1997. Like the coaches I talked to at French Lick, Gerson found that most people had fond memories of their local schools—and Friday night basketball. Gerson, who became a speechwriter for President George W. Bush, noted that while vouchers are popular among Republican policymakers in Washington, "it turns out that the grass-roots appeal of vouchers is weak even in some of America's most conservative communities."

Indianans are an "older brand" of conservative, Gerson wrote, which "more often means the love of local institutions, which do not lose public support even when they are imperfect. Public schools are valued, not because they are efficient in the sense that markets are efficient but because they are 'ours.'" More than nostalgia is at stake. Support for local schools would dissipate if they badly fail children, Gerson concluded. But since polls often show that suburban and small town parents are happy with their local schools, arguments for vouchers touting the benefits of choice and competition just don't have legs.

CHAPTER TWO

Small Schools in Big Sky Country
September 24 – October 22

Woodman School, Montana

From French Lick I would travel north past Indianapolis and into Michigan. Six hours on the road was enough, and I retired to yet another Super 8 motel. The highlight of my Michigan visit was the time I spent with two homeschooling families who left no doubt about the importance they placed on parental choice and family culture. I returned to Indiana, this time to a charter school in inner-city Gary in the northwestern part of the state. I spent my day with a teacher who had a difficult time maintaining order and motivating his students—a reminder that all the brave talk you hear from education reformers about "struggle" and "challenge" masks an often exhausting day-to-day reality.

Next I toured two Catholic schools in Milwaukee that were revitalized by that city's pioneering school voucher program. The visits provoked some soul-searching as I considered the meaning of parental choice. I tacked north and west to Minnesota's Twin Cities to visit two very different charter schools—an innovative online school and an honor-bound military academy. Both schools were passionate about their programs and intensely proud of their accomplishments. Then I traveled across the desolate openness of North Dakota, with stops at schools with religious commitments—an Adventist school near Bismarck and a Christian school in Dickinson—and then on across Montana to a modern version of an old model of schooling: students in grades K-8 studying in a four-room schoolhouse outside Missoula.

I was glad to be crossing the northern tier of states in October before Old Man Winter awakened, with Evan as a companion and a VW in good running order. We reached the Pacific Northwest somewhat faster than Lewis and Clark, one-quarter of the way through our education trek. In a plush and leafy suburb of Seattle I visited two Montessori schools and experienced the reality of the founder's concept that children learn by teaching themselves. Later in the week I was in an Oregon public charter school that practices Direct Instruction, a strictly structured group learning program that is the polar opposite to Montessori. After passing through the beautiful Willamette Valley my final visit on this leg of the trip was to another online virtual school, Oregon Connections Academy. A public school run by a private company, it is a school of choice for many homeschoolers.

September 24, 2008
Homeschooling in Central Michigan

Sam Young lives near Lansing, in a comfortable but modest farmhouse in the flatlands of central Michigan. Sam and I had scheduled a meeting at a Panera Bread restaurant in town, but after a quick conversation he invited me back to his home for dinner: "Let's grill stuff." It was a warm early fall evening, and I was glad to make the 20-minute drive along the pencil-straight road to his home.

In the Young's driveway I met the rest of the family: Mrs. Young, who was expecting the couples' fourth child; their daughter, age 10; two sons, both younger; and a litter of cats. The children were excited to show me around their back yard, and an all-family soccer game quickly broke out. After the exercise, Sam grilled hamburgers as we talked.

Sam and his wife have decided to homeschool their children. By way of explanation he notes that he is one of thirteen children—several adopted—and was homeschooled through college. After earning a law degree online, he taught for five years in Russia and made an unsuccessful run for state representative. Sam is now in his early thirties and is happy with a job in sales. He feels his homespun education has served him well.

Homeschoolers like to point out that in early America education was centered in the home. In the 1960s and 1970s, increasing numbers of parents grew disillusioned with conventional schooling and began to explore homeschooling as an option for their children. These families tended to fall into two camps: there were religious conservatives, many

27

of them inspired by the writings of Raymond and Dorothy Moore, and there was the countercultural-left, whose guru is the author and teacher John Holt.

Raymond and Dorothy Moore argued that young children form a bond with their parents that cannot be replicated by schools. Because this bond is crucial to the child's long-term success in life, they concluded that early school enrollment is not only unhelpful but can be harmful to children. They explicitly rejected "rushing children into formal study at home or school before 8 or 10 [years of age]." Work and service, they said, were essential to complement book learning.

Like the Moores, John Holt embraced an expansive view of education, but the key to his philosophy was a belief that students had to follow their own interests and "learn by living." It's a philosophy that Holt's followers have termed "unschooling," with an emphasis on discovery. Child-led learning was more important than formal lessons and school schedules. Despite their differences, both Holt and the Moores consider the home a natural institution and the school an artificial one. And both adamantly insist that education occurs not only in "school," but in the community, the church, and the marketplace: education takes place in all of life.

The Young family has a mix of reasons for homeschooling. Sam believes his childhood homeschool experience enabled him to learn how to interact more naturally with adults. Spending time with adults in a variety of settings—not just in a teacher-student relationship—is something he wants for his own kids. The Young family is Christian, and freedom to teach their children about God is a central concern. In addition, Sam knows homeschooling brought him close to his siblings, a benefit he wants for his kids.

After dinner the children went to bed while the parents and I sat and talked. The family has a TV, but only for movies. The living room bookshelves sag under heavy volumes, mostly classics and the collected works of favorite authors. Last month's phone bill was a cause for worry. Like most homeschooling families, the Youngs have made a decision to live on one income in order to educate their children at home.

Before I left Michigan Sam suggested I visit his friends, the Stensons, who are also homeschoolers. Over homemade chili the next day Mrs. Stenson told me she and her husband homeschool mainly for academic reasons. Their oldest son wasn't challenged academically at his local public school, and a second son had a hard time learning to read. The Stensons live only a few blocks from an elementary school, and Mrs. Stenson said she was troubled by what she observed year after year. Watching kids walk to school, she noticed that they began each school year with joy and energy. Children walked past the Stenson house laughing and talking. But within a couple weeks their enthusiasm waned, the smiles disappeared and the kids trudged to school. "That told me something. If that was normal, I wanted a different experience for my kids."

Unlike many observers I find nothing odd about homeschooling. Undoubtedly that's because my three brothers and I were homeschooled when we were young. My parents weren't explicit followers of either Moore or Holt; they simply wanted to guide the trajectory of their kids' upbringing, and homeschooling afforded them that opportunity in an unparalleled way. I think the ability to guide a child's upbringing is what most parents want, whether they homeschool or not. It's a parent's prerogative, and my visits to these homeschoolers not only highlighted that but provided me with a question I would use when looking at other schools: How do we set up our education system so that parents have the most robust opportunity to exercise their natural authority in guiding their child's upbringing?

September 25, 2008
Big Rock Elementary School, Chesaning, Michigan

Walking down the hallway at Big Rock Elementary School in the village of Chesaning, Michigan, midway between Lansing and Flint, takes me past rows of hooks from which little Spiderman and Incredible Hulk backpacks hang. When I think of a "normal" small town school, I think of a place like Big Rock, a public elementary school of close to 400 students located in a middle-class town.

The school allowed me to observe a 4th grade class, and I was invited to banter with nine-year olds about my trip around the country. The students asked "questions"—"Have you been to Kansas? My grandmother lives in Kansas." "My uncle lives in Pennsylvania. You should go to Hershey Park!" The conversation, so random and circuitous, was illuminating. These students had an innate curiosity and wanted to share their knowledge. But what they had to say was unstructured and haphazard. What does this mean for teaching? Great teachers balance disciplined form and free expression, analysis and instinct. Teachers must be both a "guide on the side" and a "sage on the stage." That's the reason why there is no end to the debate between ancients and moderns, classics and romantics, Aristotelians and Rousseaueans.

The most enlightening aspect of my short visit was a conversation with the school's counselor. She told me the students' most common worries are family or peer-related. Recently she had to deal with several third graders who were imitating characters in the movie "Mean Girls." The students had adopted the names of girls in the movie and formed a club to bully their classmates. For good and ill, popular culture seeps into schools.

But culture is more than movies. It includes what sociologist James Coleman termed "social capital," the "set of resources that inhere in family relations and in community organization and that are useful for the cognitive or social development of a child or young person." Strong families and strong communities produce the cultural strength that gives rise to good schools. Schools in turn build social capital, bringing neighbors together for the sake of their children. It's an important secondary function of schools, particularly in rural areas like Chesaning.

The "Mean Girls" story illustrates something else. Any one student's school experience hinges on the other students in the school. Parents are well aware of this, and when they evaluate a school, they're looking at the other kids and the kid's families. To the extent parents want control over their children's education, they care about the other children in the school. As I would come to see in subsequent school visits, this concern for *who* is in their school has important implications when parents weigh the merits of vouchers versus neighborhood public schools.

September 26, 2008
Gary Lighthouse Charter School, Gary, Indiana

The city of Gary was founded in the early twentieth century by U.S. Steel, a corporation that fell on hard times in the 1960s, laid off workers, and took the city's economy down with it. Today Gary is one of the most dangerous cities in the country. To order lunch at a Subway fast-food shop I had to give my order to a woman behind a solid Plexiglas wall and receive my sandwich through a small bulletproof revolving gate. It was unnerving and unwelcoming.

That's one reason why Rob and several other teachers at Gary Lighthouse Charter School (GLCS) would rather make a daily one hour and thirty minute roundtrip commute from Chicago than live in Gary. Since I was staying with Rob, I also made the commute.

GLCS opened in 2005 and it is in the difficult early stage of creating a school culture of high expectations and respect for learning, a culture very different from the urban street culture of the neighborhoods surrounding it. Rob said the process is extra difficult because the school opened several grades at once rather than one grade level at a time. Start with just one grade and you have a better shot at creating a new and better climate for the kids; open several grades and you are more likely to import all the problems of the community.

Maintaining order at GLCS was touch-and-go, particularly because this was a day full of distractions—a problem compounded by flooding that forced staff and students into a new building. The day of my visit was the last day of two grueling weeks of ISTEP (Indiana Statewide Testing for Educational Progress), the mandated state tests that all students take between grades three and ten. The students seemed beleaguered, unfocused and occasionally belligerent. Some needed one-on-one supervision. During the test one boy kept calling his girlfriend on his cell phone.

Creating a school's culture is tough business. At GLCS the teachers need to be comfortable wielding authority in a combative and unruly environment, which is easier said than done. Rob, just finishing his first month of teaching, admitted that he wasn't sure whether he knew how to be a disciplinarian. There were times, he said, when he truly didn't know how to respond to students, to get them to listen or focus on their work. Many students didn't take school at all seriously, and it was all he could do to keep them under control.

It's not easy to attract and retain quality teachers at schools in tough neighborhoods. It's probably an advantage for charter schools that their principals have greater flexibility with hiring and firing decisions, but that certainly doesn't mean all charter schools will have better teachers and achieve better results. They won't.

September 27, 2008—A Delay

I left Gary deeply skeptical that teachers and schools can improve kids' lives without changes in family and neighborhood. Back in Chicago I met an old college friend at the train station, a looming structure of impressive appearance, white stone set against a dark and threatening sky. I parked the car. The downtown neighborhood seemed safe enough. Following our reunion and a quick meal of hot dogs, Chicago-style (chopped tomatoes, pickles, celery salt and black pepper on top), I walked back to my car. Approaching it I noticed little nuggets of clear glass littering the sidewalk below what had been the car's rear window on the driver's side.

Two lap-tops and two backpacks stolen, and with them all my work. Distressed and angry ("Stupid!"), I called the police, who could do nothing. I sat on the curb and heard the first crack of thunder. The skies opened, and the rain came pouring down.

October 2 and 3, 2008
Two Catholic Schools in Milwaukee, Wisconsin

In 1990, the Wisconsin state legislature enacted the Milwaukee Parental School Choice Program, the first urban school voucher program in the country. Designed to provide low-income students with educational opportunities, the program was enacted with support from an unusual political coalition that would come to characterize support for urban voucher programs: Republican politicians, conservative grant-making foundations, and low-income African-American parents.

The program began modestly, and was limited to 15 percent of Milwaukee Public School students. Parents who used vouchers reported that they were happier with their students' new schools, and the program grew. In 1998, the Wisconsin Supreme Court ruled that vouchers could be used at religious schools, and the program expanded. In 2008, nearly 20,000 Milwaukee students attended about 120 voucher schools.

The effect of the program on student academic achievement—both for the students who attended voucher schools and those who remained in Milwaukee public schools—is fiercely debated, though most high quality studies of school vouchers have shown they lead to modest academic improvement for students who make use of them. In Milwaukee, one certain result has been a revitalization of the city's non-public schools, many of them Catholic. I visited two, St. Anthony's School and Notre Dame Middle School.

St. Anthony's School

It was another grey and blustery fall day, and the wind whipped up the waves on Lake Michigan. I turned the car, with its newly replaced window, away from the lake and headed into Milwaukee's south side, to St. Anthony's School, a looming square brick building.

It was calm and bright inside. With 1,000 students in grades K-8, St. Anthony's is the largest grade school in Milwaukee. In many ways it is typical of a 21st century urban Catholic school. Academic courses, student discipline and religion are taken seriously. Almost all the students come from poor households. At St. Anthony's Spanish is the students' first language. Some students are Catholic, some aren't. The students wear uniforms, which at St. Anthony's consists of white shirts and green sweaters with the school coat of arms on the sleeve. Older students must wear blazers, and outstanding students sport colored ties.

The ties aim to symbolize a culture that respects achievement. It is one element in a strategy developed during the last six years under the leadership of school president Terry Brown. As Brown explained it, St. Anthony's is "a good hybrid between a no-fluff charter school and a traditional Catholic school."

"No-fluff" has become a term for a no-nonsense approach to discipline and hard work in school. It refers to schools that set high academic standards, that relentlessly monitor student behavior and tell kids to shape up—a concept explained in David Whitman's book, *Sweating the Small Stuff* (2008). Brown referred to the book several times during our conversation. Whitman profiles six urban schools that embrace what he calls "the new paternalism." These are schools that have adopted a "broken windows" approach to education similar to the urban policy theory New York City mayor Rudolph Giuliani took in fighting crime. The premise of the "broken windows" theory is that urban areas and institutions like city schools suffer primarily from disorder. "Stop the visible signs of disorder—fix the broken window, in [sociologist James Q.] Wilson's terms—and teachers and students will regain a sense of safety and involvement," wrote Whitman. "Conversely, evidence of disorder left unattended—graffiti on toilet stalls, rowdy hallways, dirty cafeterias, students walking about with their shirts not tucked in—only breeds more disorder."

St. Anthony's was certainly orderly. Students were in class when they were supposed to be, and they were engaged with their texts and teachers in the classes I observed. When I walked into a classroom with Mr. Brown, all the students turned in their desks and faced us. Everyone. "Good morning Mr. Brown," they said. "Good morning. You may go back to your work," he replied. Sometimes the students add a "praised be Jesus Christ" to their greeting.

Perhaps more than anything else, St. Anthony's understands that a prerequisite to learning is a good school culture. "All I know is if we didn't train the kids how to behave, we couldn't have the advancements in learning," Brown said. "It doesn't matter how great the teachers are, if the culture isn't there to support them." When it's possible, school culture should complement the positive attributes of a student's family life and neighborhood. When it's necessary, school culture should supplant the negative attributes.

St. Anthony's refuses to accommodate negative attitudes and behaviors that walk through the school door. Its goal is to tie excellence in academic education to a sound moral compass. "We see what happens when really bright people don't have a moral compass," Brown said, referring to Enron, Worldcom and other scandals in the news. "Here at St. Anthony's, the moral compass comes from Catholicism." But take away the religion, he said, and "the U.S. still has the moral compass to teach people to be honest, respectful, decent and responsible."

If enrollment is any indication, St Anthony's is what many Milwaukee parents are looking for. And if St. Anthony's did not provide what parents want, they could always take their vouchers to another Milwaukee school. That's the beauty of choice.

Notre Dame Middle School

Notre Dame Middle School also has seen its enrollment increase because of vouchers. The only all-girls middle school in Wisconsin, it's just a few blocks from St. Anthony's. The school—sponsored by the School Sisters of Notre Dame—has 120 students. Classes are capped at 16 students. The girls wear uniforms and classrooms are orderly, but the atmosphere seems more relaxed and less in need of discipline. School principal Sister Jean Ellman told me she has taught in all-boys schools, all-girls schools and coed schools. "All have their place," she said, "but the biggest advantage of the all-girls environment is less distractions."

While few of the students come from "advantaged" homes, Sister Jean said they do well after leaving Notre Dame. Usually they attend one of six Catholic high schools in Milwaukee, including two all-girls high schools. But because not enough vouchers are available, some girls whose families can't afford tuition go back to public school. Notre Dame tracks its graduates and reports that 95 percent graduate from high school after leaving Notre Dame.

One reason for the schools' success may be the length of the school day. School runs from 8:00 in the morning until 6:00 in the evening. Traditional classes end at 3:30, but students are required to stay and participate in after-school enrichment programs, including sports, sewing, music and theatre. The after-school programs are largely supervised by volunteers who act in *loco parentis*. One volunteer writes, "There are three components to running a successful educational institution: good administration, dedicated teachers and caring parents who participate when necessary. Notre Dame has the first two, and although the third is difficult in some cases, it is bolstered by willing and able volunteers."

Most schools in Milwaukee would love to have the community

support that Notre Dame enjoys. What is it about this school? Partly it may be that the school is private and Catholic. In the 1980s, James Coleman led a group of researchers in analyzing the nation's largest longitudinal data-set about schools, involving 28,000 sample students attending 1,015 public and private schools. His book, *Public and Private High Schools: The Impact of Communities* (1987), laid out its findings. One was that private schools, and Catholic schools in particular, had more social capital—good will, trust, a sense of obligation and responsibility among and between the individuals comprising the school community. Coleman believed the higher level of social capital was one reason why Catholic school students tended to outperform public school students from similar backgrounds.

Notre Dame and St. Anthony's illustrate the potential of vouchers to lift students out of public school systems that do not serve them well. Still, the voucher program has not had the transformational impact on public schools that their advocates anticipated. The theory was that public schools would be forced to improve in order to compete with private schools that received vouchers. But there have been no large-scale improvements in the Milwaukee Public Schools. And many voucher schools aren't that much different from city schools. An account by reporters from the *Milwaukee Journal Sentinel* concluded: "The voucher schools feel, and look, surprisingly like schools in the Milwaukee Public School district. Both...are struggling in the same battle to educate low-income, minority students."

Because the voucher program is restricted to private schools *within* Milwaukee (St. Thomas More High School, a private Catholic school near St. Anthony's but just outside the city limits, cannot take part in the voucher program) and because the city's school children are overwhelmingly poor and minority, it's not surprising that voucher schools resemble city public schools.

Parental Choice vs. Parental Choice

I think "peer effect" is an important reason for the academic success of students in the Milwaukee voucher schools. The more motivated parents enroll their children in charter schools and voucher programs. And when strongly-motivated students go to school with one another, it's much easier to establish the positive academic culture that St. Anthony's Terry Brown identifies as the prerequisite for student learning.

Consider another Milwaukee program known as Chapter 220. It is a long-running voluntary desegregation program that allows 5,000 African-American students to be bussed from the city to suburban public schools. (Several thousand more are on a wait list.) Professors James Ryan and Michael Heise note that a legislative audit of the program "found that minority transfer students performed better on statewide achievement tests than minority students in the Milwaukee city schools, including those students who tried to transfer to suburban schools but were unable to." In other words, busing helped.

Ryan and Heise found that highly motivated students had a positive spillover effect on their peers whether through the self-selection taking place at many charter schools and voucher schools, or when low-income urban students are bused to suburban schools full of middle class kids. However, the authors concluded that voucher programs would be more modest in their effect when they were restricted to students within city limits.

Ryan and Heise found that suburban parents and homeowners were wary of a robust inter-district voucher program and worried that inter-district vouchers would produce an influx of minority city kids with family and neighborhood problems. Wanting to protect their public schools, suburbanites believed voucher programs would undercut their control over their children's education. (I explore suburban fear of universal state-wide voucher programs in Chapter 6 in the context of school voucher ballot initiatives in Utah and California that were rejected by voters.)

This realization was slow to dawn on me. It's really what's behind what I think is at the heart of the debate over where kids go to school: Parental choice—the ability of parents to choose the schools they want their children to attend—is at odds with parental choice—the ability of parents to choose the kids who will go to school with their children in neighborhoods located where they choose to live.

October 8, 2008
General John Vessey Jr. Leadership Academy,
St. Paul, Minnesota

I stewed on the questions raised by the Milwaukee voucher program over a weekend with relatives in Dodgeville, Wisconsin. I was glad to have something to think about instead of the Chicago theft of my belongings. The following Monday I was off to Vessey Leadership Academy in St. Paul. Minnesota.

Vessey is a publicly-supported charter high school built around the U.S. Army's Junior Reserve Officer Training Corps (JROTC) program. When I walked in the Vessey schoolhouse door the first thing I learned was the Cadet Creed:

I am a Vessey Leadership Academy JROTC cadet.

I will always conduct myself to bring honor to my family, country, school, and Corps of Cadets.

I am loyal and patriotic.

I am the future of the United States of America.

I do not lie, cheat or steal and will always be accountable for my actions and deeds.

I will always practice good citizenship and patriotism.

I will work hard to improve my mind and strengthen my body.

I will seek the mantel of leadership and stand prepared to uphold the Constitution and the American way of life.

HOOAH!!!!

Vessey opened in 2004 with 72 students, but now serves 120 cadets—60 percent male—from the Twin Cities area. Three retired military personnel are on staff; the rest are civilians. I spoke with Sgt. Major Don Vance, a retired Army officer and the school's executive director. The students call him Sergeant Major. He told me that Vessey grew out of a popular after-school program that addressed serious gang issues in East St. Paul.

One of each day's six periods of class is devoted to JROTC. The students in class were in uniform and stood in formation for inspection by a student leader. They did pushups for infractions of discipline or for failing to comply with proper dress standards. A color guard carries the flag during visits by military officers and dignitaries, who have included President Lech Walesa of Poland and retired U.S. General Tommy Franks. Leadership and responsibility are important components of the school's philosophy.

Vessey students come from across the Twin Cities area, and while many join the military, the majority make other career and education choices. The Academy makes no effort to connect itself with the culture of its students' old neighborhoods. Indeed, many students are eager to escape their old neighborhood and want no part of it. Instead, Vessey tries to create a new ethos centered on personal honor, loyalty to the corps, and patriotic duty to country.

October 8, 2008
Bluesky Charter School, St. Paul, Minnesota

Vessey is a St. Paul public charter school and so is Bluesky, but the surface similarities end there. Forget what you know about school. Forget the buses. Forget the fire drills and the school lunches. No more study hall, no more peer pressure or school dances. In fact, no more school building.

What's left is "pure education," says Tom Ellis, Director of Bluesky Charter School. Some of us would find it painful to imagine high school without these facilities and experiences. But to others it sounds like a pretty darn good idea. It's for them that Bluesky exists.

Bluesky is a 100 percent online school, the first in Minnesota. Upwards of 80 staff members and teachers serve more than 800 Bluesky students in grades 7-12. As with any public school, there is no tuition cost for state residents seeking a Bluesky education. Teachers are licensed—most taught in "brick and mortar" schools before coming to Bluesky—and the school's curriculum meets state requirements. But that's where the similarities end, says Ellis. "If we aren't different, then there is no reason for us to exist."

At its offices in West St. Paul I listened as eight Bluesky teachers spoke passionately about the benefits of going to school online. Some benefits are immediately apparent (flexibility in time and location; custom-tailored instruction) but others are counterintuitive: the teachers said they build close relationships with students who feel safer and can better express themselves online.

Students come to Bluesky "because they don't have much hope for themselves or their futures," one teacher told me. There are lots of teen moms. "You think these women feel welcomed and at home in a traditional school? I don't think so," said Ellis emphatically. "Here, many of them feel comfortable in school for the first time." Ellis said teen moms are the school's most successful students.

Getting Bluesky started wasn't easy, but now that it's been growing rapidly other schools like it are starting to attract students across the country. An astounding 750,000 students now "attend" online public schools. That's just under one percent of the total school population, and a five-fold increase since the 2001-2002 school year.

Vessey and Bluesky aren't for everyone, and a student who wants to go to Vessey is unlikely to want to go to Bluesky (and vice-versa). But they are examples of an amazing diversity in schooling that public charter schools are making possible.

October 9, 2008
Dakota Adventist Academy, Bismarck, North Dakota

It still has a Bismarck address, but it's 17 miles north of the state capital and no aspect of urban life is visible on the campus of Dakota Adventist Academy. I was in for an experience in austere education in a rugged land. The school sits alone on 850 acres amid North Dakota's vast rolling hills where Lewis and Clark once passed. The hills are covered in tough grasses on which a few cows graze, hemmed in by barbed wire fencing. Tumbleweed was swept along by a chill autumn wind. The landscape is impressive and suggestive of author Thomas Hardy's description of the rural England countryside he called Egdon Heath: "singularly colossal and mysterious in its swarthy monotony. As with some persons who have long lived apart, solitude seemed to look out of its countenance."

The solemnity of its geographic location is mirrored by the atmosphere of Dakota Adventist Academy. Brick walls and a coal boiler shelter 51 students from the wind and cold. The school only recently made arrangements for Internet reception. In a large circular and dimly lit common room at the school's entrance I watched as a young girl silently moved a cloth in slow circles, polishing a Plexiglas railing. This was the most subdued school I visited. "It's stable and safe here," said David Chapman, the administrator and teacher who showed me around. "It gives [the students] a safe place to learn about God."

The Academy is part of the school system run by the Adventist Church. Adventists have their roots in the Millerite movement of the 1830s and early 1840s, which became famous for William Miller's prediction that the Second Advent of Jesus would occur on October 22, 1844. When that failed to occur and after a reexamination of the Scriptures, the Church was formally established as the Seventh-day Adventists in 1863. It has over 15 million members worldwide.

Adventist education began in 1872 with a mission "to provide opportunity for students to accept Christ as their Savior, to allow the Holy Spirit to transform their lives, and to fulfill the commission of preaching the gospel to all the world." Adventists today have the second largest Christian school system in the world, after Roman Catholics. Over 7,000 schools and colleges serve nearly a million and a half students worldwide.

Dakota Adventist Academy (DAA) fulfills the Church's educational mission in North Dakota. In this predominantly rural state there aren't enough families in close proximity for a day school; DAA operates as a boarding school for students from all corners of the state. The boarding school model also complements the Adventist belief that Saturday is the Sabbath. In other communities social activities are concentrated on Friday night and Saturday, but at DAA, "The edges of the Sabbath hours are to be carefully guarded," the school's handbook instructs. At the Academy the students are all on the same schedule and so don't feel isolated and ostracized. "We have the advantage," said Chapman, "of being able to bring kids together with similar beliefs."

Adventist beliefs extend beyond Saturday Sabbath. Alcohol and tobacco are strictly forbidden, as are the unclean foods identified in the Scriptures: The DAA cafeteria is vegetarian, and caffeine is discouraged. Other regulations in the handbook: "Caps may only be worn outdoors and in the shop"; "hair color should be of natural tint"; no icons, logos or written messages in opposition to Christian principles; no "disseminating ideas that are in opposition to Seventh-day Adventist beliefs or undermining ideas and policies of the school by continuous criticism." It sounds severe, but Adventists aren't looking for sympathy as James R. Nix wrote in *Growing Up Adventist: No Apologies Needed*

"Though it seems unbelievable to some, I'm thankful that when I grew up in the church [in the 1950s and 1960s] I was taught not to go to the movie theater, dance, listen to popular music, read novels, wear jewelry, play cards, bowl, play pool, or even be fascinated by professional sports."

Chapman showed me the school's expansive view from a floor to ceiling window in the second floor cafeteria. The Missouri river is nearby, while far in the distance I could see steam rising from two coal plants— a booming industry in North Dakota. The school recognizes the need to instruct students in their duties as citizens and it provides cultural and historic contexts for learning, but Chapman said the principal focus is on eternity: "We want our kids to go to heaven." DAA is more than a school, "it's a lifestyle."

It's hard for me to relate to the Adventist lifestyle, and its philosophy of education is too distinctive to fit into a public school system—not that the Adventists want that. They are happy not to have the strings that are attached to government funding and are satisfied to offer a school environment for Seventh-day Adventist families.

I was not invited to observe DAA classes or meet its students.

October 9, 2008
Hope Christian Academy, Dickinson, North Dakota

From Dakota Adventist Academy I hopped onto I-94 and drove at the 75 mph speed limit to Dickinson in the western part of the state. Ron Dazell, Director of Hope Christian Academy, invited me to the school's first annual "community appreciation" night. There was coffee and cake for parents and school supporters, he said, and I could get a feel for the school and community.

HCA is housed in one of the town's evangelical churches, and tuition is remarkably low—about $2,300. Dazell told me the school firmly embraces the idea that "parents are primarily responsible for the education of their children," and that schools and teachers exist to assist them. Before first grade, HCA hopes students will remain at home with their parents. As a Christian school, HCA's mission is to reinforce the "Judeo-Christian values that Christian parents strive to teach in the home."

Dazell noted that all textbook publishers write from a perspective, citing disputes over curriculum that are never-ending and cover all subject areas. There are the math wars, reading wars (phonics vs. "whole language"), pedagogical wars over "traditional" vs. "progressive" learning, and culture wars over the content and teaching of history and literature. Dazell said he tried to select publishers whose Christian outlook corresponds to his values and to the values of the parents who choose HCA.

Education scholar Diane Ravitch has said independent schools like HCA are attractive to many families because their texts don't have the "strong tone of cultural resentment" that pervades "bowdlerized" mainstream textbooks. Mainstream publishers strip away descriptions and details from their texts because they are afraid of giving offense to this or that group. An excess of political correctness deprives mainstream school texts of much of their content, especially in history and literature courses.

While private schools like HCA give parents an alternative to mass-marketed textbooks, they also send strong signals to public schools about what families and communities value. Ravitch says it's not enough to say that every family, group or community should get to choose the type of American history and literature consistent with its beliefs. That's an evasion, not an answer to the battles over school curriculum. Ravitch says Americans share a culture that is worthy to be taught.

"For how, in a society as varied and rapidly changing as our own, can a common culture survive without a clear commitment to broadly shared standards for the teaching of literature and history? And absent any such shared culture, how can we communicate across lines of race, religion, ethnicity, and social class in order to forge common purposes?"

In our democracy the problem lies in defining those "broadly shared standards." We make our choices as citizens when we vote for office-holders who will set public school policies. But citizens can also vote with their feet. They can move to another school district or state, or enroll their children in private school or homeschool them.

I could see that the cafeteria was filling with people for community appreciation night. Dozens of men and women approached me to welcome me to their school, and as I sat in their pleasant company two HCA graduates now in the Dickinson public high school described the principal lessons they learned at HCA: They were taught to think for themselves and to stand up for their convictions. They were comfortable professing their faith as Christians.

In a cafeteria in Dickinson, North Dakota, the curriculum wars that serve as stand-ins for culture wars did not seem quite as intense and angry. It occurred to me that this is because these parents had built a community with others who shared their values and expectations. One more lesson I was learning on this trip: People cluster with others like themselves when they choose the community in which they want to live, no matter whether they send their children to a private school or a public school. It is how they create the environment they want for themselves and for their children.

October 13, 2008
The Woodman School, Lolo, Montana

From North Dakota through Montana and into Idaho, wherever I went, Lewis and Clark were there first. States are eager to advertise their historic presence. Rest areas are built where the explorers rested. Little brown signs dot the roadside, pointing out "areas of interest:" Pull over to see where Lewis and Clark clashed with Indians. Check out where Clark built a canoe. Lewis carved his name on a rock over here. It was certainly only a matter of time before a sign called me to see where these famous Americans paused to relieve themselves.

To get to the Woodman school you drive nine miles from Missoula, in west-central Montana, to Lolo, once a rough-and-tumble gambling outpost portrayed in the movie *A River Runs Through It*. Turn right at the third stoplight and drive nine more miles on US 12 toward Lolo Pass between Montana and Idaho in the northern Rocky Mountains. The school sits partway up the sloping bank of a valley formed by the Bitterroot River. When I arrived the solid grey sky was giving way to mixed sun and clouds. Some grassy hills were drenched in sun. Other slopes were dark with pines, with patches of snow underneath.

Visiting the Woodman School in Montana surely felt like a trip back in time. Every year the school invites an elderly alumnus to speak to its students about times past. An accomplished storyteller, he shares tales of digging through snow in a blizzard to reach the school's outhouse and the wolves that came down off the mountain to harass the cattle. The outhouse is long gone, but wolves still do come down and mess with the beef. Last year the entire student body gathered in the driveway to watch a wolf chase the cattle until the herd realized there is strength in numbers, turned, and drove off the lone intruder. It isn't difficult for all the Woodman students to congregate in the driveway: There are only about 50 of them. Many students are siblings, and more still are members of extended families.

Woodman is not quite a one-room schoolhouse; it houses grades K-2, 3-4, 5-6, and 7-8 in four classrooms. In the 19th century most Americans went to one-room schoolhouses. In 1917, there were still 196,000 one-teacher public schools in the United States. Today the number is only several hundred, but 80 are in Montana. Woodman's enrollment fluctuates, peaking at 79 one year in the 1960s when the highway workers who built Lolo Pass brought their kids with them. Woodman's size allows, indeed *requires*, parents and teachers to know one another and work closely together. There is no administrative bureaucracy standing in the way.

"We heard the cattle guard, so we knew you were here," a teacher told me when I arrived. "Perhaps I missed him," I responded. Oops. A cattle guard isn't a man in uniform guarding cattle, but a grate in the road across which the cattle have trouble walking. They're everywhere in the rural West and much appreciated by ranchers, though not by the struts of my tired, heavily-laden station wagon.

I went into the K-2 class first, where the teacher read a story about "The Biggest Bear." Several students had brought in traps, including a bear trap, and were demonstrating how they worked. At recess the entire student body played football. Next I went to the combined 7-8th grade civics class where students described growing up in Lolo. One girl explained how rumors spread. "There's a rumor that the teacher went skinny dipping with the students down in Lolo Creek," she said with excitement on her tongue and a mischievous gleam in her eye.

Students fish and hunt, but rodeo is what gets the most attention.

They all go to it, and several girls are very good riders. When I said I had never seen a rodeo, the girls' jaws hit the floor. Easterner.

G.K. Chesterton wrote, "Education is simply the soul of a society as it passes from one generation to another." At Woodman the soul will need to absorb the three Rs, bull-riding and fly-fishing. Students will also learn about wolves and cattle and how their parents and grandparents lived. Those things provide context and meaning, the glue that holds communities together.

October 16 & 17, 2008
Eton School and Bellevue Montessori School,
Bellevue, Washington

The kids were everywhere and they were all doing something different—some stacking blocks or studying map-puzzles, others pouring water into buckets or counting beads—and all using smartly designed and colorful educational materials. The Eton School's structure of individualized learning, from the decentralized work stations to the assortment of "learning tools," was the embodiment of a Montessori school.

Montessori schools are inspired by the teaching method and philosophy of Maria Montessori. "An amazing woman, Maria," everyone at the school informed me. She was a devout Italian Catholic, a physician and educator who worked with mentally disabled and poor children in Rome in the early 20th century. Her achievements were sometimes called a "miracle" and the model for her schools spread over Italy. After fascist Benito Mussolini came to power in 1922, he confined and then exiled Montessori for refusing to change her schools to meet his demand for warriors and mothers of warriors. Montessori lived and worked in Spain, the Netherlands and India before her death in 1952.

The central pillar of the Montessori philosophy is that young children teach themselves through a process Montessori called "spontaneous self-development." While guidance and the right environment are necessary, Montessori believed children have an innate appetite and aptitude for learning. She considered the type of instruction that ordinarily occurs in traditional school classrooms more hindrance than help. Teachers of young children should be observers and guides, not lecturers. Learning can be effortless and joyful, said Montessori, if the materials are right and the timing is natural.

In Washington State there are close to a hundred Montessori schools, including dozens in the Seattle metro area. I visited two in Bellevue, an upscale suburban area full of comfortable homes and office parks, on the verdant, rainy Eastside of Lake Washington.

Patricia Felton is founder and current director of Eton School. As we toured the school, Felton explained the Montessori view that it is critically important for the youngest children to use concrete "hands-on" materials; learning is connected with doing, the brain with the hand. Instead of relying on a teacher to give them correct answers, children can learn to correct their own mistakes using specially designed Montessori materials. I observed students working independently on activities in one of the five work areas prescribed for all Montessori schools: Practical Life (tweezing, buttoning, pouring and working on other small motor skills), Sensorial, Math, Reading and Cultural (botany, zoology and geography). The method embodies the Montessori philosophy of "responsible freedom in a controlled environment."

Christine Hoffman, the director of Bellevue Montessori School, made a similar point. Her school maintains an environment that rewards initiative and concentrated effort. Students have the flexibility to decide when and for how long they will pursue an activity. "If we see concentrated effort," she said, "we'll let it go as long as possible." To "let it go" builds the child's attention span. This fits Montessori's belief that children learn most often and best during periods of intense concentration. In a 2004 television program on the ten most interesting people of the year, Google founders Larry Page and Sergey Brin—both Montessori-educated—attributed part of their success to the fact that they were encouraged in school to be self-starters.

Eton and Bellevue serve a pretty special demographic. The schools are located across from the headquarters of Microsoft, and many of the students' parents work for the computer giant. Microsoft scours the world to find the most talented employees, and the school's racial diversity is a reflection of the large number of East and South Asian engineers and computer scientists who work for Microsoft. These parents are super-involved, and "when parents have a concern," Felton said, "it is, 'can the kids go faster? Can the school be more challenging?'" Lakeside, where Bill Gates went to high school, is a sought-after destination for students graduating from Eton.

By many measures, both Eton and Bellevue are successful schools. The students do well and their parents are involved. Teachers and staff feel connected to the schools' mission and culture. As Felton said, "We all look at kids the same way." Felton—a product of the Catholic school system and a former public school teacher—recognized that Montessori wasn't the only way to give schools a common culture and mission. "I imagine parochial schools are similar in this way," she said.

These Montessori schools reinforced a consistent message that I've picked up on at all the schools I've visited: Schools function best when teachers and parents agree on their mission. For parents who seek a particular school curriculum or philosophy of learning, the key is to find others who share the vision.

October 21, 2008
Reynolds Arthur Academy, Troutdale, Oregon

What follows is an example of the unusual teaching method used at the seven Arthur Academy public charter schools. It's called "Direct Instruction."

Good morning. My name is Mr. Brand. Today you are going to learn about the Reynolds Arthur Academy. The first topic we are going to discuss is: location of the school.

My turn. The first topic is: location of the school.

When I signal, I want you to say, "location of the school." When I signal by writing "signal" in bold I want you to say, "location of the school." The topic is: location of the school.

Your turn. What's the topic? Get ready. **Signal.**

That's right: location of the school. The location of the school tells where the school is. Where is the school?

My turn. Where is the school? The location of the school is: Troutdale, Oregon.

Your turn. When I signal you say, "Troutdale, Oregon."

Where's the school? Get ready. **Signal.**

That's right, the school's location is Troutdale, Oregon.

The second topic we are going to discuss is...

This method of teaching seems to be a very drawn out way to say that the Reynolds Arthur Academy is located in Troutdale, Oregon. Collective repetition, however, is part of the design at this K-5 charter school. As I watched Chris Arnold, the school manager and one of the kindergarten teachers, go through a phonics lesson for 5-year-olds seated around her on the floor, I realized the method was grounded in *rhythm*. The dialogue moved regularly between her and the students: instruction, a question, a signal, a group response and brief congratulations for a correct answer or immediate correction of a false one. Chris worked deliberately through a stack of flashcards with letters and letter combinations, making sure the students knew the sound each made.

Charles "Chuck" Arthur, the current director of the school, started the first Arthur Academy in 2002 because he felt the local public schools lacked a coherent and effective curriculum, which was preventing kids from achieving their potential. When Oregon's charter school law was passed in 1999, Arthur saw an opportunity to start a school where he could implement a curriculum of his choice.

Arthur said he likes to think of his method as "incremental mastery." Students proceed along sequenced paths of instruction in small steps toward a larger goal. Their progress is regularly checked, and they don't move on until mastery of the component parts is achieved. "It's the best one," said Arthur, comparing Direct Instruction to other curriculums and methods. Students are engaged, there aren't any gaps in their understanding, and students' confidence rises as they see themselves learning and doing well on mandated state tests.

Arthur, who taught in the Oregon public school system for 30 years, is very supportive of Oregon public schools. But he was disappointed that the public education establishment and the general public were unwilling to appreciate the benefits of Direct Instruction: "We're old school, and get frowned upon sometimes for it." People think DI is too narrow, but "there's more to it than just a traditional approach to the three R's." Arthur believes DI can work in almost any school environment, but he admits that teachers must want to teach that way for the technique to work. Most teachers simply will not buy into the curriculum, which means the program cannot be implemented.

Arthur welcomes the charter school concept as a way to give public schools more independence, which allows for a diversity of approaches. Parents who are looking for a Direct Instruction education for their kids now have a place to send them.

October 22, 2008
Oregon Connections Academy, Scio, Oregon

Forty-nine days on the road and I am now in Oregon's beautiful Willamette Valley, which runs north and south between the coastal mountains and the Cascades. The town of Scio is in northwest Oregon, a half hour southeast of Salem, the state capital. The drive down from Seattle took me through rolling hills past miles of vineyards. The region's winters usually aren't harsh enough to bring snow, and the climate is excellent for growing grapes.

The school I was visiting, Oregon Connections Academy (ORCA), is another virtual school. Its offices were tough to find tucked behind a coffee shop in this town of 700. ORCA is part of a larger network of schools governed by Connections Academy, a for-profit online education provider based in Maryland.

Like BlueSky Charter, the online school I visited in Minnesota, ORCA is a high school that serves students struggling to graduate. However, ORCA also enrolls one-third of its students from another important demographic: Families who previously homeschooled their kids. "We get students who were homeschooled, or whose siblings were homeschooled, whose parents are looking for more support, more help," said principal Jerry Wilks, an imposing figure who once played professional football with the Pittsburgh Steelers.

Keeping up with each student's individualized program is one of the challenges of teaching in a program like ORCA, said Reese, one of the school's teachers. Without seeing kids every day, teachers lose the physical cues to gauge student needs and progress that they would have at a brick-and-mortar school. A good rapport with parents really helps, but "parents sometimes have a hard time seeing weaknesses in their children," said Reese with a laugh, so a very active virtual presence is required.

As a public school principal for many years, Wilks witnessed the limitations of that environment. "I saw students walk out of my office and I had nothing else to give them," he said. He knows that Connections Academy certainly isn't for everyone. It's too rigid for homeschooling families who are used to more freedom in the curriculum and schedule, while for other families it demands too much involvement.

"I don't think it will ever replace, and I don't want it to replace, the brick-and-mortar school. Nothing will replace that," Reese said, and Wilks agreed. Face-to-face peer and teacher interaction, school activities from sports to theater, and the overall sense of community created by many schools is hard to simulate in an online environment. Reese's three children attend a local public school, and Wilks spoke highly of public schools in the Scio district. But Connections Academy provides a "real viable alternative," he said, and he points to the rapidly growing enrollment—more than 3,000 students next year—as evidence of that. Oregon Connections Academy—a public school run by a private company—demonstrates that public-private partnerships, including online ones, can be effective in providing public education.

CHAPTER THREE

Across the Great Plains
Timeless Wisdom and Magnet Schools
October 24 – November 21

Masonry student in West Virginia

Diverse as my experiences have been, I was starting to settle into a comforting routine: Visit a school in the morning, drive to the next destination in the afternoon, and write about the morning's visit at night. Entering the third month of my travels, I was glad to be driving east in the afternoons with the sun's glare no longer in my eyes.

First stop: Moscow, Idaho, where I watched a film of "Henry V" with high school juniors from the Logos School, a Christian school using a "classical education" curriculum. The kids didn't mind that we were watching Shakespeare in the teacher's living room on a Friday night. Next: a public school in Casper, Wyoming. Under the city's open enrollment policy Casper parents have the option to send their kids to any public school no matter where they live. The Casper Classical Academy is a public school that also offers the classical education curriculum—Latin, logic and the liberal arts.

Then it was on to South Dakota's Pine Ridge Indian Reservation, where the effort to preserve traditional Indian culture is frustrated by the realities of contemporary Indian life. I spent a disquieting Halloween night in a town on the reservation's outskirts. That was followed by a visit to a public school in White Lake, South Dakota, whose principal raised a question that I would return to several times on this trip: Who should decide how much money is spent on public education?

In Omaha, Nebraska, I toured a private Catholic school in the Cristo Rey network, which uses an innovative work-study program to prepare students from low-income families for high achievement in college. I then went to public magnet schools in Omaha, Nebraska; Louisville, Kentucky; and Charleston, West Virginia. In this section I have added accounts of my subsequent visits to magnet schools in Kansas City and St. Louis. Magnet schools were used to end racial segregation and they help foster school choice, but their critics charge that they weaken neighborhoods, encourage extravagant school spending, and fail to achieve the goals they set for themselves.

In Iowa I went back to my old grade school, where I once meditated among the corn and soybean fields, and in Illinois I learned some lessons about and from Abraham Lincoln. A visit to a Chicago charter school was a reminder that school politics in big cities is not for the faint-hearted.

It was now almost Thanksgiving and a chill was in the air as I drove through the Blue Ridge Mountains on my way to a masonry shop at a vocational technical high school in Martinsburg, West Virginia. I had to wonder whether parents who push their children to attend college are doing what's best for them.

October 24, 2008
Logos School, Moscow, Idaho

The University of Idaho is in Moscow, and its football team had a home game. That meant the town was flooded with parents and alumni who booked all the hotels, and that meant I was sleeping again in the back of the station wagon. I was awakened in the morning by scraping sounds on the pavement. I couldn't see the snowplow because the night's snowfall had blanketed my windows.

On Friday night high school teacher Bob Vance invited 25 juniors in his Rhetoric class over to his house for a movie. Every year, after his students read Shakespeare's *Henry V*, Vance has them watch Kenneth Branagh's 1989 film version. Vance and his students are from Logos School, a K-12 Christian school that opened in 1981 with 18 students housed in a rented church basement. Logos now has 250 students, and it's considered a leader in the burgeoning movement for classical education.

What is classical education? Logos' founders are inspired by a 1947 essay, "The Lost Tools of Learning," by the English novelist Dorothy Sayers. Sayers argued that there was something seriously amiss in modern education with its emphasis on specific and isolated bits and pieces of knowledge. Schools, she urged, needed to adopt "the mediaeval scheme of education…what the men of the Middle Ages supposed to be the object and the right order of the educative process." At the heart of this "classical education" was the trivium, whose three parts are Grammar, Dialectic, and Rhetoric. The trivium was used for the study of Latin but Sayers said it actually instructed pupils in the process of learning. First, students learn grammar (hence, grammar school) "what it was, how it was put together, and how it worked." Then they learn dialectic, or how to construct an argument and detect fallacies. Finally, the pupil studies rhetoric, or how to use ideas clearly and persuasively. Sayers said these steps—the building blocks of knowledge—apply to all fields of study, not just language.

Sayers believed the trivium helps structure a K-12 school because its three stages correlate to a child's development. The youngest child engages in rote learning by memorizing and reciting. As children grow older they start to contradict and answer back. They like "to 'catch people out' (especially one's elders)." Finally, self-centered and expressive adolescents reach the third stage, where the child "rather specializes in being misunderstood; it is restless and tries to achieve independence; and, with good luck and good guidance, it should show the beginnings of creativeness."

The Logos model offers both a theory about how children learn and a philosophy about the proper ends of education. That means phonics and arithmetic drills for the younger children, courses in logic and debate team for older ones. The curriculum at Logos (Greek for "the word") makes use of original documents and "great books" such as Shakespeare's plays. Bob Vance, who teaches Rhetoric, says, "We use Aristotle, we use source documents a lot in classical education." Vance says the classics are studied and criticized from a Christian perspective.

After showing the film, Vance and his students discussed its themes of loyalty and bravery ("We few, we happy few, we band of brothers..."), then milled about the living room as a line of parents' cars formed outside. Most Logos parents work in agriculture or for the University of Idaho, the two largest local employers. Annual tuition for the school averages $3,700.

As I spoke with Mr. Vance and munched on homemade rice-crispy treats, I was reminded of something else Dorothy Sayers wrote about education. Sayers' view was that problems in modern education are byproducts of cultural confusion. What I've seen on this trip convinces me that Sayers is right. What and how you learn in school reflects the priorities of the larger society. Culture precedes and shapes schools. Mostly that means the culture of the community where the school is. At Logos, it means Shakespeare on a Friday night.

October 29, 2008
Casper Classical Academy, Casper, Wyoming

"The day is done, and the darkness

Falls from the wings of Night,

As a feather is wafted downward

From an eagle in his flight."

The girl who murmured the opening stanza of this Longfellow poem was one of 28 students in a seventh grade English class at Casper Classical Academy (CCA). Public speaking is part of the school's curriculum and that means reciting poetry in front of your classmates. Principal Marie Puryear knows the name "Casper Classical Academy" conjures up images of an elite private school, but it's a misconception. CCA is a public middle school in a city of 50,000, the second largest in Wyoming. It offers students a classical education curriculum, requiring classes in the arts, Latin, logic and political discourse as well as more typical core subjects.

This being Wyoming, not everything is classical in the Greco-Roman sense. I attended a "learning new things" class to start off the day. During a session devoted to Outdoor Survival, students learned how to tell if a bear is angry and ready to attack, how to repair a tent, and how to remove a fishhook from your cheek.

Puryear explained that CCA was founded because local parents wanted a place where their children could receive a "back-to-basics" education of high academic standards, structure and discipline. The Natrona County School District recognized the demand and, not wanting parents to start a charter school, responded by instituting an open enrollment policy. The district, which serves about 12,000 K-12 students in Casper and surrounding towns, has become a "district of choice."

As a district of choice, parents may enroll their child at any one of the 34 public schools in the county, subject to limits on capacity. Where a child lives does not determine where he or she goes to school as it would in a neighborhood school system. Instead, each school can develop its own curriculum or school policy, and parents can choose the one they like best. According to the district, "The diversity among schools has provided opportunities for each child to learn in his or her unique way and for parents to become more involved."

Natrona County has had open enrollment and schools of choice for over a decade, and a majority of students now attend a school outside their residential neighborhood. But the move to open enrollment hasn't been universally welcomed. Many Casper residents would like to return to neighborhood schools, and even CCA, which would not exist without open enrollment, thinks the case can be made for more neighborhood preference.

The criticisms of public school open enrollment are many: busing students costs too much; it's ridiculous to make a student go across town because the school next door is full; the neighborhood community is weakened; parents get to "cherry pick" their child's school, creating a stratified system of good and bad schools. Puryear told me some city residents had hard feelings when Casper first opened: They blasted the school as "just for doctors' and lawyers' kids."

I'd bet that CCA does have lots of doctors' and lawyers' kids. When parents have similar educational goals for their children it's only natural that they organize and create schools that fit their needs and desires. But neighborhood schools can have the same effect. On this trip I've seen how neighborhood public schools create their own purposes— and their own social stratification, one based on residency. Where you live determines who you go to school with. As for losing a sense of neighborhood community, Puryear says schools of choice also create a sense of community: "If we were a neighborhood school, it would defeat the whole purpose of our school, and destroy community and parent buy-in." One teacher pointed out that after CCA opened its doors the county's public school enrollment actually increased because local homeschooling families realized there was now a public school that shared their values.

How do you calculate the advantages of neighborhood schools against those of schools of choice? Nobody wants a school system where a first grader has to be bused across town because there are no spots left at the elementary school across the street. But it makes little sense to require that students go to a neighborhood school when one further away better serves their needs. Parents should be able to send their sons and daughters to schools that work for them. In Casper, the system of open enrollment appears to be offering parents that choice.

October, 31, 2008
Red Cloud Indian School, Pine Ridge, South Dakota

Pine Ridge Indian Reservation is in the southwest corner of South Dakota, two hours from Mt. Rushmore. The Oscar-winning movie "Dances with Wolves," which portrayed battles between Sioux Indians and the U.S. cavalry, was filmed near the reservation, which is also close to the site of the 1890 Wounded Knee massacre. The reservation is home to some 20,000 Native Americans and is larger in size than the state of Delaware. It is also one of the most impoverished areas of the country. Unemployment hovers above 75 percent; life span is lower and child mortality higher than the national average. Alcoholism is rampant.

I wanted to visit an Indian school because I had read about the evolution of public attitudes and government policies toward Indian education. In the early years of the 20th century, government agents and missionaries tried to remove Indian children from their native cultures. They gave Indian children haircuts and dressed them in store-bought clothing. Only later was greater respect paid to Native American history and culture. Interested in seeing for myself how these changes were carried out in practice, I visited Red Cloud Indian School.

Founded by the Jesuits in 1888 at the invitation of Chief Red Cloud, leader of the Oglala Sioux, the school was originally called Holy Rosary Mission School. But in 1969 the name was changed to honor the great chief and emphasize the school's respect for Native American culture. Tina Merdanian, a Red Cloud graduate and now director for institutional relations at the school, gave me a tour, beginning with the chapel. She said the benches were made of pine from the nearby Black Hills, a place spiritually sacred to the Sioux. The stained glass windows were patterned after Native American artwork. And there are paintings on the chapel wall that depict Jesus as a Native American—and the Romans as U.S. cavalry.

The Sioux in South Dakota are called the Lakota, and the school's 600 students study from a curriculum focused on Lakota culture, Lakota religion, and Lakota language. Though Red Cloud is a Catholic school, Merdanian said students' identities come largely from their Indian culture and the school is working to preserve Indian history. She concluded my short tour in the gift shop, which has Native American crafts and artwork for sale.

After leaving the school and its invocation of the Indian past, I drove through what is today the Pine Ridge reservation. A vast plain, it is dotted by trailers and clusters of cars, many of them broken and abandoned. The sun set on the prairie and the last rays of light faded. Twilight was an appropriate setting for what I was seeing.

Just beyond the reservation, I stopped for a sandwich at a hole-in-the-wall pizza and sub shop containing two soda coolers, a plywood counter and a couple freezers. The Indian woman behind the counter watched soap operas on a mini-TV suspended from the ceiling. It was a clear and chilly Halloween night. As I leaned against the wall waiting for my order I watched groups of teenage Indian boys dressed in baggy black pants wander down the otherwise deserted street. They entered the store to buy liters of Coke and Dr. Pepper. Mostly Dr. Pepper. Some of the younger kids were in Halloween costumes. They were not dressed as Indians.

November 4, 2008
White Lake School District, White Lake, South Dakota

When I stopped the car for a stretch-break, I noticed pheasant remains—feet and feathers—scattered along the side of the road. Then in White Lake, a town just off I-80 in southeastern South Dakota, I saw men everywhere dressed in orange and camouflage. It was pheasant hunting season. "You would be surprised," White Lake School principal Burle Johnson told me, "at how many kids have shotguns in their car trunks."

Like many public schools in the upper Midwest, White Lake has a student body that scores well on academic tests. Every year since 2002 the school has met standards for progress under the No Child Left Behind law, and in 2006 White Lake was named a blue ribbon school for high achievement. But the White Lake school district faces some tough challenges because there aren't enough jobs in the area to hold young people. Enrollments are slowly declining, a problem faced by many small town schools, and demographic decline means less funding. These trends have prompted the White Lake school district to join a statewide funding lawsuit. Johnson said it's the biggest issue he has faced in forty years in education.

In 2006, 59 South Dakota school districts, including White Lake, filed a lawsuit against the state, claiming that the education finance system was failing to provide sufficient resources to give students an "adequate" education. To make its case, the South Dakota Alliance for Education—an advocacy organization for school districts, school boards, school administrators and the state teachers union— commissioned a cost study to prove that state school funding was inadequate. The report concluded that South Dakota schools were under-funded by an amounted estimated at from $133 million to $400 million. While the test scores for White Lake schools are clustered near 100% proficiency, the school district's funding was deemed to be more than $700,000 short of "adequate."

I learned that it's not just in South Dakota where schools sue their state for more money. "For three decades," writes Stanford education professor Eric Hanushek, "state school funding has been driven by a series of court cases concerned with fiscal equity." There have been lawsuits challenging state methods for funding public schools in 45 of the 50 states, and many have been ongoing for decades.

The South Dakota lawsuit didn't make sense to me. Certainly courts should ensure that schools abide by provisions of the state constitution, but I question how they can make detailed finance decisions. What number—$133 million? $400 million?—guarantees an adequate education? Who's to say White Lake must have another $700,000?

Despite the views of panels of "experts," why can't citizens, speaking through their elected officials, decide how much money they should spend on their schools? I will discuss this issue in greater detail in chapter 4.

November 8, 2008
St. Peter Claver Cristo Rey Catholic High School,
Omaha, Nebraska

In 1965 one in eight American children was educated in a Catholic school. Not anymore. Catholic school enrollment has declined from 5.2 million in 1960 to 2.3 million students, and the number of Catholic schools is only half of what it once was. Today Catholic schools enroll less than one in 20 students.

The rising costs of education are certainly among the primary causes for the decline of Catholic school systems. Many low-income families feel they can't afford to pay Catholic school tuition when they are already paying taxes to support public schools. But in Omaha, Nebraska, the founders of St. Peter Claver High School think they have found an answer. The high school, one of 22 schools nationwide that are members of the Cristo Rey network, funds its operations through an innovative work-study program. The result is a secondary school that puts learning in the context of faith, offers low-income students rigorous academic courses, and is building a self-sustaining funding mechanism.

The innovation at the Cristo Rey schools is the network's Corporate Internship Program (CIP), which makes every Cristo Rey high school an employment-leasing firm. CIP contracts with local businesses to find meaningful work experiences for its high school students. Employers—banks, law firms, hospitals, and consulting firms—receive the services of entry-level employees, while student/workers earn income to pay their tuition. Students work one day a week and make up lost school time with a longer school day and school year. The Corporate Internship Program at St. Peter Claver pays for about 75 percent of each student's education costs. Annual student tuition—$1,825—accounts for another 10-12 percent, and fundraising provides the rest.

Father Jim Keiter, the school's principal, told me he plans to add 125 students next year and hopes to grow the school to 500 students. To cover its capital costs, the school still needs to fundraise. On the day I visited St. Peter Claver was holding an annual dinner and benefit fundraiser. Attracting hundreds of church members, parents and teachers, employers and other community members, the school raised several hundred thousand dollars from a silent auction, and raffled off a new car. I won a signed PGA golf cap.

It's hard for private schools to prepare ambitious low-income kids for high-achieving futures while they pay the bills. The Cristo Rey network is pioneering one solution.

November 7, 2008
Spring Lake Magnet Elementary School, Omaha, Nebraska

Omaha developed in the late 19th century as a railway and transportation hub. It built stockyards, then meatpacking plants, and hired immigrants to work in them—Irish, Poles, Czechs, Lithuanians, and Italians. More recently, the city has seen an influx of Hispanic and Sudanese immigrants.

Spring Lake is one of 15 public magnet schools in Omaha's 80-school system. It's a fast-growing elementary school on Omaha's south side and currently enrolls nearly 700 students. Magnet schools get their name from the idea that schools can attract students from across residential boundaries if they are large and offer comprehensive facilities and special opportunities in particular subject areas like technology or math. The argument often made for magnet schools is that bright students receive educational opportunities they would not get at neighborhood schools.

However Omaha's magnet schools have a different purpose and a different history. They were the preferred alternative to school busing and were established to reduce de facto minority segregation. The school district, Omaha Public Schools (OPS), says its magnet schools are part of a plan to create a "learning environment that embraces diversity and cultural understanding."

With that goal in mind the Omaha board of education divided the district into four zones. Each zone ties parts of the mostly minority eastern section of the city to the mostly non-minority west end. Within each zone parents can choose to send their child either to an assigned neighborhood school or to a magnet school.

Spring Lake is part of the Orange Zone "pathway" that in theory allows a Spring Lake elementary student to move forward to other magnet schools like Marrs Middle School and South High School. However, principal Susan Aguilera-Robles told me that magnet schools have not achieved their goals. Robles, who enrolled her own children in both public and private Omaha schools, explained that almost all Spring Lake students come from the surrounding neighborhood.

I'm not surprised that Omaha magnet schools haven't achieved their goals. As I've discovered, many parents simply prefer to have their own children go to school with their neighbors' kids in the communities where they live. Like other magnet schools I would visit, they seemed to have little impact on America's racial divide.

November 10, 2008
Maharishi School of the Age of Enlightenment, Fairfield, Iowa

Fairfield is a town of 10,000 people in southeastern Iowa, and like many Iowa towns it is surrounded by corn and soybean fields. I lived in Fairfield in the mid-1990s when I was nine and ten, but had not returned till now. Looking for my old house, I followed the county road five miles past town, took a left and drove another mile until I came to what looked like Juniper Avenue, my old street, a rutted dirt path whose topsoil would cling to my shoes. Our old house wasn't where it should have been. All that remained was a hedge of small pines that once marked the edge of our yard.

The old farmhouse was gone, but in town I could see the two large golden domes where many residents practice transcendental meditation. Fairfield is home to the Maharishi University of Management and Transcendental Meditation. It combines Midwest farm traditions with new age Eastern spirituality, which makes Fairfield a town unto itself.

In 1959 the Indian spiritualist Maharishi Mahesh Yogi ("great seer" in Hindi), guru to the Beatles, brought Transcendental Meditation (TM) to America. His form of meditation is intended to help its practitioners reduce stress and achieve inner peace. The meditation technique is quite simple. You sit with your eyes closed for 20 minutes while silently repeating a mantra. TM practitioners say meditation acts as a form of deep rest, energizing the body and clearing the mind.

Maharishi's followers incorporated meditation into the classroom at the K-12 school they established in Fairfield, the Maharishi School of the Age of Enlightenment (MSAE). The school's founders believed education's problems—academic underachievement and learning and behavior issues—are rooted in stress. "The pressures and stresses a child faces as he or she navigates the often treacherous corridors of student life...can inhibit the development of a still-developing brain..." said Ashley Deans, the head of MSAE. To overcome these pressures the school proposes meditation and a "consciousness-based" approach to education.

The school philosophy begins with Maharishi's thoughts on education: "There are two sides to knowledge: the object of knowledge, that which we seek to know, and the subject of knowledge, the knower." Because most education systems focus on the contents of knowledge, the curriculum, rather than on the needs of the knower, the student, "the whole structure of knowledge is as if baseless." Though we may ignore it, the connection of the learner to himself is at the heart of learning. MSAE emphasizes the age-old maxim, "know thyself." And by emphasizing techniques of meditation, it focuses on the physiological aspects of learning. The school is a unique place: Its "hall of bliss"—the fourth floor covered in white carpet—accommodates the students, who meditate twice a day, learn Sanskrit and "Vedic math," and take more traditional courses.

Naturally there is some town-gown tension between the school and skeptical Fairfield locals, but admissions director Tere Cutler told me there is also growing acceptance. She said, "We reach out to them where they are," which means through sporting events and giving support to local businesses. She also emphasized that the assistance is reciprocal: the school draws on the values and resources of the small Iowa community. I talked to a class of eleventh grade boys who reported mixed experiences in interacting with local public school students. Some had close friends in public school, but one boy said he was punched in the face once it was known he was a meditator, or "roo" (short for guru).

While most parents wouldn't consider enrolling their own child in the MSAE school program, they would surely recognize that their kids are susceptible to the pressures and anxieties that MSAE aims to reduce. Young people buckle under the weight of broken families, violence, unsafe schools, drugs, peer pressure, boredom, and exhaustion. Even successful students know the pressure of "going Ivy."

I attended MSAE in fourth and fifth grade, before my family moved to upstate New York. I also played Little League and soccer with the town kids. There was definitely some animosity between the two groups, but no great rift. Tere Cutler retrieved from the school's files a letter I wrote when I was nine years old. I had been homeschooled and was about to attend MSAE. I wrote that I looked forward to interacting with other kids and teachers beyond my immediate family. It was as simple as that.

Looking back on these experiences, what surprises me most is that I recall my years at MSAE as perfectly ordinary. Meditation, single gender-classes and learning Sanskrit seemed completely normal at the time. Only now do I appreciate the uniqueness of my education and the value of those experiences.

November 12, 2008
Noble Street Charter School, Chicago, Illinois

The process of education reform in Chicago, writes University of Santa Clara law professor Steve Diamond, has been a constant struggle between two groups: corporate and foundation elites, who think they can reform Chicago schools with outside money and expertise, and local community groups, who want grassroots activists to launch a schools takeover.

When Chicago public schools were on the brink of collapse in the late 1980s—U.S. Secretary of Education Bill Bennett called them the "worst in the nation"—the two reform factions temporarily united. Spurred to action by an unpopular teachers' strike in 1987, the Illinois legislature radically decentralized school governance. Local School Councils were created and were given the power to hire and fire principals. That cheered the activists, who wanted to create, in Diamond's words, a "new power center in the school system against what both reform groups viewed as the bureaucratic and expensive school board, on the one hand, and, on the other, the teachers union."

Not every one was on board. Many African American professionals in Chicago were alarmed by school reform. They thought it was a way to quash the unions and control school administrators, "both institutions where Chicago blacks had, finally, after many decades of exclusion, found secure middle class careers." They also worried that proposals for local control would open the door to charter schools and other ideas opposed by the teacher unions and the education establishment.

The reform factions parted company as the local schools councils fell into disarray in the mid 1990s. On one side was the Annenberg Foundation, which announced a major philanthropic initiative. It would give $50 million in challenge grants to improve Chicago public schools using a proposal co-written by education professor Bill Ayers. The Chicago Annenberg Challenge proposed to strengthen and expand the local schools concept. On the other side, Chicago Mayor Richard Daley pushed for more mayoral authority over the city's schools. The two camps were moving in opposite directions: While the Annenberg Foundation poured millions into selected "Annenberg schools," the Mayor was moving to take over all the schools. Both sides postured to get their way. The upshot was that the local school council idea was retained, but the Board of Education was restructured so that the Mayor had all the power, exercised through a newly created position of schools CEO. Professor Ayers became a flashpoint for controversy in 2008, when his radical past was linked to his association with Barack Obama, a board member of the Chicago Annenberg Challenge.

Noble Street Charter School is a product of that turbulent debate. Unfortunately the entire state of Illinois has only 39 charter schools. (Washington, D.C. alone has 57.) Founded in 1999 by two Chicago public school teachers, it is located in West Town, an area of Chicago near Wicker Park. Like many inner city charter schools, Noble Street hammers home the message that school culture matters. High expectations, uniforms and strict discipline create a highly structured environment. Students and staff alike subscribe to a health and fitness code, and students must pass all their classes each year to move to the next grade. The school doesn't promote kids who just spend their year at a desk.

Charter schools like Noble Street have benefited from contending approaches to education reform. While they receive support from foundation and corporate outsiders, they also enjoy parental support. But they do not fit into the political and ideological boxes sometimes drawn by education reformers. Low-income and minority parents who want reform sometimes clash with unions and those who benefit from the status quo. And the business community, which chafes at the inefficiency of the central school bureaucracy also decries the messy squabbling of local school board activists. Who's ox is gored? Conservatives and liberals alternately praise local control and central control, then switch sides when their opponents take over.

Charter schools like Noble Street must navigate these sometimes dangerous currents. Meanwhile a "relentless focus on college" is what motivates the staff and inspires the students. Nearly 85 percent of Noble Street students go on to college. Because the school has a longer school day and school year, Noble students receive 25 percent more classroom time to improve their math and reading skills.

November 13, 2008
Learning Like Lincoln, Springfield, Illinois

Driving south through Illinois, I paused in Springfield, the state capital, to check out the new museum dedicated to Abraham Lincoln, the city's most famous resident. Busloads of gawky eighth graders noisily elbowed their way into the museum's cathedral-ceilinged entry hall for tours of Lincoln lore, and walked through a replica of the one-room log cabin where young Abe read before the fireplace.

Our nation's 16th president received little formal education. Of his childhood, Lincoln recalled that he attended "some schools, so called," though the time he spent in the classroom would barely fill a school year. His learning was self-taught and drawn from a small stock of books that included the Bible, Aesop's Fables and the works of Shakespeare. In 1852, Lincoln eulogized Henry Clay in a way that others would repeat in describing his own life: "Mr. Clay's lack of a more perfect early education, however it may be regretted generally, teaches at least one profitable lesson; it teaches that in this country, one can scarcely be so poor, but that, if he will, he can acquire sufficient education to get through the world respectably."

When he ran for the Illinois General Assembly in 1832, Lincoln summed up his views on the purpose of education in what might be considered his first press release.

"Upon the subject of education, not presuming to dictate any plan or system respecting it, I can only say that I view it as the most important subject which we as a people can be engaged in. That every man may receive at least, a moderate education, and thereby be enabled to read the histories of his own and other countries, by which he may duly appreciate the value of our free institutions, appears to be an object of vital importance, even on this account alone, to say nothing of the advantages and satisfaction to be derived from all being able to read the scriptures and other works, both of a religious and moral nature, for themselves."

Lincoln lost the election.

November 18, 2008
Louisville Male Traditional High School, Louisville, Kentucky

Twin spires rise from the grandstand of magnificent Churchill Downs in downtown Louisville. There were no horse races that Tuesday, but I was able to walk around the legendary track, famous for hosting the Kentucky Derby. On the first Saturday in May, 150,000 spectators watch "the most exciting two minutes in sports" and drink Mint Juleps on the massive lawn beside the track. The race—first run in 1875—and the drink are Kentucky traditions. Just outside of Louisville I drove past some of the country's most famous bourbon distilleries: Makers Mark, Wild Turkey, Jim Beam.

Louisville Male Traditional High School has deep roots in the city, and its history reflects some of the city's divisions by academic attainment, gender, class and race. Principal Dave Wilson explained that the letter "H" proudly displayed around the school and plastered on school paperwork stands simply for "High School" – no further designation was necessary when the school was founded in 1856 as the only public high school west of the Alleghenies. Its origins go even further back to the Jefferson Seminary, a public academy that received its charter from the Kentucky General Assembly in 1798, only six years after Kentucky became a state.

But Male had a reputation for academic elitism and it was challenged by a new high school—DuPont Manual—established in 1892 "to provide young men with a system of education which would fit them, in a more direct and positive manner, for the actual duties of life." Male and DuPont Manual, one academic, the other technical, held their first football game the following year, beginning one of America's longest-running high school football rivalries. Male won the first game 14-12.

Many people wonder about the school's name, Wilson said. Male considered changing it when it went co-ed, but female students liked the brand name because it was a signal of the school's reputation for excellence. Today, Louisville Male is 60% female.

There is also the matter of race. The schools I've been visiting across the northern tier of states from Minnesota and the Dakotas to the Pacific Northwest tend to be mainly white. But going to Louisville reminds me that racial division plays a central role in American education. Desegregation was late in coming to Louisville. City schools were not integrated until they were forced to do so by a federal injunction in 1975. The Ku Klux Klan demonstrated and white protestors attacked school buses carrying black students. The injunction ended only in 2000 when Louisville adopted its own desegregation plan, requiring every school to have from 15% to 50% black students.

Both busing and magnet schools played a key role in Louisville's desegregation planning. With 100,000 students, 35 percent black and 55 percent white, Louisville looked to its four magnet high schools to draw in students from different parts of the racially divided city. The city also bussed students from their homes to schools across town. (Wilson said the city spends a fortune busing its kids 86,000 miles a day all over the city.) As a magnet school, Male is supposed to be open to anyone in the city. But Louisville's magnet program has a system that begins in elementary school and carries over to students at middle and high schools. Students who participate in the "traditional" program— academic rigor, dress codes, an emphasis on civics and patriotism—are entitled to priority admission to Male. Male typically doesn't have room for applicants outside the pipeline—the school is already 200 students over capacity.

Counting by race in Louisville—and across America—is entering a new phase. In June 2007, the Supreme Court ruled 5-to-4 in *Meredith v. Jefferson County School Board* that Louisville's efforts at promoting racial integration violated the 14th Amendment's equal protection clause. Chief Justice John Roberts wrote the plurality opinion: "The way to stop discrimination on the basis of race is to stop discriminating on the basis of race." Race is now only one of ten mainly socioeconomic factors used to assign students to schools. Principal Wilson hasn't seen the practical impact of the Supreme Court's ruling yet. He did say the gap in grades and test scores at Male isn't between black and white students, but between rich and poor. By mandating a shift in focus from race to social class, the Court is perhaps on to something.

Wilson is convinced that Louisville Male High School is not about race or class. It's about scholarship, patriotism, loyalty, courtesy, respect, responsibility, and citizenship. Students at Male take pride in their school. "It's like a throwback to 30 or 40 years ago when kids 'belonged' to their school," said Wilson. He told me about times when he would put a cup of water in the middle of the gym during assemblies and tell students to make it shake by their yelling and stomping. And last year Louisville Male students set a world record in setting off Mentos and diet cola geysers. (It's true: I saw the video.) "School spirit" activities, removed as they may seem from actual learning, help students at Male build a relationship with their school. Male understands that citizens value schools for more reasons than formal education or the prospect of a higher income.

November, 20, 2008
George Washington High School, Charleston, West Virginia

My GPS navigator doesn't understand what makes for enjoyable driving. It takes me places by the shortest route, even if that means sharp turns down bumpy back roads or hectic highway merges just to "save" two minutes. But in West Virginia obscure shortcuts are appreciated. The road I took brought me winding in the afternoon sun through a green residential district set on a hillside overlooking Charleston, the state capital, before curving down alongside the Kanawha River towards the golden dome of the Capitol building. It was a short but scenic drive that left me with a good feeling about the place.

My positive impression of the area continued during my school visit to George Washington High School (GW). GW is part neighborhood school and part magnet school; three-fourths of the students live near it, but others participate in its Advanced Placement magnet program. Qualified students can select GW, or one of eight other magnet schools in the Kanawha County school district, regardless of where they live. As a result, GW sees a range of students from diverse socio-economic and academic backgrounds. "We have kids coming from the projects," said vice principal Valery Harper, but also some with the highest test scores in the state. Sixty percent of students take at least one AP class.

It was a busy day for Harper: two of the school's four administrators were absent and Thanksgiving Break was approaching. I was glad for the opportunity to talk, but as soon as I sat down the phone rang and

Harper was dashing off. She returned moments later to resume our conversation holding a Ziploc bag of marijuana confiscated from a student. GW has a unique organization, she explained, more like college than high school. It's called "modular structure" scheduling, developed in the early 1960s in collaboration with Ohio State University to produce "self-directed learners."

Harper's remarks were interrupted by a walkie-talkie call about what appeared to be a parking issue. No sooner was this resolved when a lunch lady came in with questions. A coffee pot was broken; should they get another? The fall semester parent-teacher conference was that evening: How many cinnamon buns should she make? Requisition the pot. Three trays will do.

Back to our conversation: "The school is really in a transition period," she said. Students don't always make good use of the unstructured time the school's unique scheduling system provides. GW has added a mandatory "GW 101" freshman course to explain the system and prepare younger students for the school's expectations.

Harper looked quizzically at a student who arrived at the doorway to her office. "I sweated it out," he said, grabbing at his drenched t-shirt. He'd forgotten to bring a change of clothes to gym class. She directed him to where he might find a replacement.

All of a sudden a girl suffering a panic attack came to Harper's office. She had left class and called her grandpa who was coming to school to comfort her and bring her food—she hadn't eaten breakfast. The girl did-n't want anyone to think she was skipping class. Harper assured her that she wasn't in trouble and insisted she have a juice box.

The disruptions might leave an impression that GW is a school out of control, its administrators putting out fires all day long. But I didn't get that feeling; the problems arising seemed "normal" for a large group of energetic high school students. Harper was busier than usual, but the activity lent energy and vitality to her work. I asked how she liked being vice principal. She said it was great. You ought to consider it, she told me,

"There is never a dull moment." Sure, the school is sometimes hectic and always imperfect, but so is the world that will greet its students when they graduate.

April 13, 2009
St. Louis and Kansas City, Missouri

My visits to magnet schools got me thinking. As a way to produce racial integration, their effect was marginal. What I found interesting was the parallels I saw between magnet schools and school choice. Like charter schools and schools in open-enrollment districts, magnet schools break down the familiar system of neighborhood assignment. Yet the specially-themed schools and additional spending on magnet programs too often failed to attract many students across neighborhood lines. Nowhere was this point driven home more than in Kansas City.

Between 1985 and 2003 a Missouri district court mandated that the Kansas City Metropolitan School District (KCMSD) spend over $2 billion more on its schools in order to achieve racial integration. As an alternative to forced busing, the court ordered that the money be spent to build magnet schools, boost teacher pay and revamp the city's educational offerings. It was one of the largest and most costly judicial experiments in the history of education. It failed.

The case began in 1977 when the city school district filed a suit against the state of Missouri and the suburban districts surrounding Kansas City. The suit alleged that they "had caused and perpetuated a system of racial segregation in the schools of the Kansas City metropolitan area." The city school district proposed a plan for metropolitan-wide busing. The plan proved unsatisfactory, however, after the U.S. Supreme Court ruled that city school districts could not conscript children from the suburbs into a forced busing program. Public opinion was also against busing; a 1977 *Kansas City Times* poll found 75% of residents opposed it, including 87% of whites and 61% of blacks.

The result was that the district court required that every high school and middle school and half of all the city's elementary schools become magnet schools, i.e., schools with a special focus that accept students from anywhere in the city or suburbs. Magnet schools, writes Joshua Dunn in his book about the case, were "supposed to draw in white suburban children into the KCMSD and improve the academic performance of black children." The new schools were often housed in extravagant buildings with exotic features like giant swimming pools and planetariums. One school even hired a Russian Olympic fencing coach for its students.

Despite the exaggerated measures, "Student achievement fell and the percentage of minority students increased." What went wrong? According to Dunn, parents thought the magnet program was too complex and many "suspected that all these special programs might actually get in the way of their children's education." They didn't help educationally disadvantaged students because they were designed for kids from educationally advantaged backgrounds—who didn't show up.

Another problem, says Dunn, was that magnet schools "often created a two-tiered school district with academically gifted white and black students attending a few magnet schools while the majority of students remained in racially isolated and poorly performing traditional schools."

The judge in the case, Arthur Benson, later said, "We believed that if you put together a science school you will attract kids and their parents who are truly interested in science and are turned on and enthusiastic about science and you will attract teachers over time." To his surprise, that didn't occur. Students "selected schools on the basis of where their friends were going to school" and "teachers didn't want change." However, the "underlying problem," writes Dunn, was a misreading of what school characteristics are important to parents: "Most suburban parents who were supposed to be enticed to send their children to KCMSD schools were more than satisfied with their children's current schools."

The failure of judicial intervention and the magnet program led the U.S. Supreme Court to release KCMSD from court oversight in 2003. The district returned to a policy of neighborhood schools, although the experiment left a legacy of under-enrolled magnet schools and unwanted programs across the city. Many schools were forced to close.

The story in Missouri's other large city, St. Louis, is much the same. On my way through St. Louis I visited Baden Elementary, an old brick building showing signs of neglect in a poor section of the city. St. Louis also had a large and expensive court-ordered desegregation program, which included magnet schools but also busing. St. Louis enrollment plummeted too, from over 100,000 in 1970 to 30,000 for 2007-08. "Concurrently," according to the district's 2007 improvement plan, "poverty has risen among the families who send their children to public schools. Today, more than 85% of the District's students receive free or reduced lunch and over 7,000 or 20% are defined by the state as homeless." In 2009 the St. Louis school board voted to close 17 of its 85 school buildings. Baden Elementary was one of them.

The return of neighborhood schools is an ironic coming-home for desegregation policy. In the original desegregation case, *Brown v. Board*, Linda Brown, the plaintiff after whom the case is named, was fighting for the right to attend her neighborhood school. But as it turned out, neighborhood schools didn't mean integrated schools. "Cities' prior resistance, combined with residential segregation," writes Dunn, "made neighborhood schools look like yet another attempt to elude desegregation." Now, after decades of heavy-handed but ineffective judicially mandated alternatives to neighborhood schools, they're back.

When Kansas City turned to the national government and the courts to fix the city's education problems, writes Dunn, it "prompted a backlash and calls for local control from the very group the courts were supposed to be helping. The case provides a powerful—and perhaps culminating—example of the judicialization of politics and administration in the second half of the twentieth century." Intervention from on high only strengthened the desire for local control and responsibility.

November 21, 2008
James Rumsey Technical Institute, Martinsburg, West Virginia

"All my life I've always wanted to be somebody. But I see now I should have been more specific." Ken Gray

I walked into a large, open room. The walls weren't decorated or adorned, but brick chimneys in various states of completion rose up from the concrete floor on all sides. The tallest was waist high. The school day was over and it was quiet there, but I could imagine the sound of trowels scraping up mortar and smoothing it onto newly set bricks like chalk on a blackboard, but much thicker and wet.

The concrete-floored room is actually a masonry workshop at James Rumsey Technical Institute in Martinsburg, West Virginia, a small town an hour and a half northwest of Washington, DC. Most of Rumsey's students are juniors and seniors from seven area high schools. A smaller number are adults and "reverse transfers:" people with four year college degrees who have come back for career education. Rumsey is a tuition-free public school for area students that also charges adults by the class. Besides the classrooms where students study English, math and science, I toured a professional kitchen, machine shop, masonry workshop and the full automotive repair bay.

Principal Vicky Jenkins said the school atmosphere is more mature than a traditional high school. "It's calmer here. We treat them like adults and they rise to the challenge." The students spend much of their time not only outside a classroom, but outside school—at internships and in apprenticeships with local businesses. Apprenticeships remove students from the artificial environment of high school and mix them in with adults, some of whom become their role models and mentors.

Jenkins believes it's important to integrate academic and vocational education. But she is disturbed by the ever-increasing push for college preparation that she has seen during her 20 years at Rumsey. Students and parents nationwide are choosing "college prep" programs of study. The push for more advanced education may seem to reflect our changed economy, which demands it. But have we pushed too far? Jenkins sees problems with the "college or bust" mindset. "The biggest thing is that people think you can't be a success if you don't go to college, and that's too bad, because it's just not true, and it doesn't work for everyone."

The latest data on higher education suggest that the student shift into college prep programs is not all to the good. Increasing numbers of college freshman have to take remedial classes, and there are more college student drop-outs. According to current figures, fewer than sixty percent of freshman entering four year colleges graduate within six years.

Young people are drifting into and out of college at the same time that there is a serious shortage in skilled labor. Ken Gray, a retired Penn State professor and former superintendent of the VoTech high school system in Connecticut, identifies what he calls the "quiet dilemma," that stems from the mismatch between teen aspirations and economic/ labor market realities. Many graduates work in jobs that don't require a college degree. He thinks they would be better off to transfer to a technical college for one or two years to learn a marketable skill.

"This unfounded enthusiasm for college is deeply rooted," writes Gray. But he admits that an attempt to convince families that college may not be a good idea for their kids is "probably quixotic."

CHAPTER FOUR

Education along I-95
Band, Basketball, Busing and
a Weekend with the Amish
December 9 – January 15

School buses, South Boston

Contrary to those who urge us to choose only the best, I am learning that choices involve trade-offs, sacrificing one good for another. In the thick of winter I trekked north to a public school in tiny Houlton, Maine, just a mile from the Canadian border. The school prides itself on its first rate orchestra and band. How much does that contribute to making it the good school parents should want for their children? Back in Boston I stood on the steps of the former South Boston High School, the epicenter of the debate a quarter century ago over using forced school busing to remedy racial segregation. An elderly man with painful memories of the busing policy questioned what was gained and what was lost. I also visited one of Boston's new charter schools, an example of the city's policy to promote diversity through "controlled choice." In Connecticut I visited wealthy Greenwich and poor Bridgeport. The contrast prompted me to think again about whether equalized school funding is the answer to educational disparities between and within communities.

In economically depressed Pawtucket, Rhode Island and Newark, New Jersey, I chatted with kids who were hard-pressed to escape their troubles. School could be their refuge and even their salvation, but it could also be a disheartening reminder of the failures of community. On a wickedly cold night in Newark, I stepped into a public library several blocks from where race riots once rocked Bergen Street to hear "library children" describe the gangs that disrupt their middle school education.

Contrast Newark to Lancaster County, Pennsylvania, which is a few hours and light-years away. I spent a weekend with an Amish-Mennonite couple in the heart of Amish country and heard a schoolteacher extol Mennonite education as a robust example of local community control. But local public schools in Chester County, Pennsylvania, and Pine Bluff, Arkansas, surrendered community control to increase their school funding. Was the gain worth it?

December 12, 2008
Houlton High School, Houlton, Maine

"You are 1.67 miles from Canada where you sit," Houlton High School principal Marty Bouchard told me. That didn't come as a surprise; with light snow falling, it had been a 6-½ hour drive north from Boston—past Kennebunk, summer home to former president George H.W. Bush, and past Augusta, the state capital, further north and east to Bangor, then two more hours after Bangor, driving through evergreens and snow.

Houlton, the northernmost stop on I-95, is a town of 6,500. As with most small towns, those in northern Maine are losing population—but not Houlton, a border town. After September 11, 2001 the U.S. Border Patrol ramped up its operations, bringing jobs and families to the area. The town's other principal employers are a hospital, an assisted living facility and Houlton High School.

Like other school officials on this trip Principal Bouchard wanted to talk about testing. We agreed that the push for more testing and accountability is fueled by worries that other countries are outperforming the U.S., especially in science and math. U.S. student performance is mediocre in science and math literacy, according to two often-cited international tests (PISA and TIMSS), even though we spend more money per pupil on primary and secondary education than just about every other country.

However, Bouchard argued against using academic achievement in Asia as a benchmark for success in life in the United States. In Asia family expectations and social pressures influence student test scores and the structure of the education system, which is characterized by longer school days and school years. By contrast, greater freedom is built into the typical American school system. That's a good thing, said Bouchard, but one that has its own trade-offs.

Bouchard echoed many teachers and principals when he scoffed at No Child Left Behind and called its requirement of 100 percent student "proficiency" an unrealistic fantasy. He said the law would not improve students and schools and told me his teachers are frustrated and stressed-out by it requirements.

Later I spoke with three Houlton High School seniors who also were unconcerned about international competition. One was a Houlton native and the others were daughters of border agents who moved to the area after 9/11. All three were going to college and they praised their high school. "It's a small town, and people say sometimes there is nothing to do, but it was a good community to grow up in," one told me. They all agreed that the school's most impressive achievement was its band. With over 100 student members, "We dominate everyone!" they said.

A school band may not be the best way to measure academic achievement, but it gave these students a sense of participation in something important and made them proud of their school. That positive outlook can make a big difference for teachers who are trying to overcome student "attitude." My visit to Houlton High reminded me that most American schools are rooted in the local culture, and the expectations of the culture influence the quality of the school. Unlike Washington education policy experts, most parents and citizens value these connections and will not give them up.

December 12, 2008
South Boston High School, Boston, Massachusetts

In 7th grade I was the first kid picked up by the school bus. As I struggled to get ready, my brother was glued to the window, and when the bus headlights came around the bend and over the hill, he would call into the kitchen, "Phil, the bus is coming! Here comes the bus!" As is the case with brothers, his warnings were often calculated to be premature. Today, "The bus is coming" is a running joke between us.

The school bus is no laughing matter for residents of South Boston. It's a symbol evoking painful memories.

Boston, 1974

Few Boston students went to integrated schools in the early 1970s even though two decades had passed since *Brown v. Board*, the U.S. Supreme Court ruling that said separate was not equal. To little effect, Massachusetts had passed a Racial Imbalance Act in 1965, specifically outlawing racially imbalanced schools (i.e., more than 50 percent minority). Then in 1974 U.S. District Court Judge W. Arthur Garrity Jr. looked at Boston schools and found them guilty of "segregative intent."

Garrity's remedy was forced integration. He mandated that white and black students and teachers be bussed to each other's neighborhood schools. The cross-town swap would involve half the sophomore class and the entire junior class in two schools, Irish-Catholic South Boston High and black Roxbury High. Located in Boston's poorest and most insular communities, the schools were considered among the city's worst.

The school district tried to implement the court order, but South Boston High was forced to close after angry mobs surrounded the buses bringing in black students. It reopened only after metal detectors were installed. Hundreds of state police were assigned to patrol the school for three years.

The explosive reaction to the court order provoked a nationwide debate. Civil rights leaders accused "Southie" whites of racism, but busing opponents countered that Garrity's order excluded Boston's wealthy white suburbs. They lashed out at the judge, accusing him of using their children for a social experiment.

In a 2005 interview black community organizer Lewis Finfer recalled South Boston's outrage: "'Why do our children have to get bussed and why can't we go to a neighboring school, and why do kids in suburban areas get to go to neighboring schools? Why is it wrong somehow—why are we racist because we want our kids to go to neighboring schools?'"

Finfer writes that many blacks in Boston were also troubled. "I think the African Americans mostly were, 'We want better education for our kids.' I'm not sure if they were hugely for busing. I think they were more for the perk basis, 'If we want better education and busing can give us a better education, we're for it, but if there were other improvements that could be made to schools in our own areas, we'd be for that too.'" Early polls showed only bare majorities of blacks favored the policy. A 1982 Boston Globe poll found 79 percent of black parents with children in the public schools preferred an open-enrollment plan to busing.

By the time Garrity surrendered control over the schools in 1988, the Boston public school (BPS) district had shrunk from 93,000 to

57,000 students. White families pulled their kids out of Boston public schools, enrolled them in private schools or moved to the suburbs. "White flight" forced the courts to reduce the minimum threshold for what would constitute an allowable racial balance from 50 percent to nine percent white.

Painful Memories

It was cool and blustery as I walked up G Street to what was once South Boston High. The four-story yellow brick building had been subdivided into three theme-based public high schools: Excel (focused on media technology), Monument (criminal justice and public safety) and Odyssey (environment). Behind the building is a steep bank leading to a grassy knoll known as Dorchester Heights. The Heights commands an impressive view from Boston Harbor to downtown. It was here during the American Revolution that George Washington's artillery forced the Redcoats to retreat. A stone monument commemorates the victory.

At a small bakery below the hill, I spoke with Patrick, a lifelong South Boston resident and 1946 graduate of South Boston High. He confessed that education in his day was nothing special. "I just kinda got through it." He didn't know why the school was split into three. "I guess they can pay three different principals," he said sarcastically, a grin floating across his face.

Mostly Patrick had memories of the busing. "It was terrible," he said, a painful look in his eyes. "It didn't help blacks or whites. It wrecked the community." He shook his head. "It wasn't about education at all." Before the busing, if kids had a problem, their parents walked to school and took care of it. Then, "kids this high," he put his hand two feet above the ground, were shipped across the city.

The loss of control is a feeling community organizer Finfer remembers well: "I could feel—just remember feeling how much anger and powerlessness and wanting to act that people were feeling about the court decision," he recalled.

The powerlessness wasn't rooted in race or class, but in the loss of authority. Who was in charge of children and their education? The anti-busing movement was dominated by women, mostly stay-at-home moms who thought it only natural that they control their children's lives. Busing constituted a gross assault on their authority because they took it for granted that their children would attend schools near their homes. There was no busing when sociologist Robert Nisbet wrote *The Quest for Community* in 1953, but the court-ordered policy fit his view of how the modern state supplants families and neighborhoods in setting boundaries and rules. Nisbet lamented this assault on "natural authority." Lacking authority, institutions like the family and the neighborhood crumble.

South Boston High was once a center of neighborhood pride. "Young boys and girls," writer Matthew Richer observes, "were eager to grow up and play sports or cheerlead for their local schools. The annual Thanksgiving Day "Southie-Eastie" football game between South Boston and East Boston high schools was an age-old ritual, attracting crowds of more than 10,000." Patrick, the gentleman I met at the bakery, still recalled those games. Busing had destroyed the neighborhood's sense of community by telling parents that their concerns were irrelevant.

My conversation with Patrick had a powerful and lasting effect on me. When he spoke of busing, his face looked tired, his shoulders slumped. Maybe life does that to man. But maybe the court had drained an energizing force—call it personal and communal responsibility, or simply human agency—from lives in South Boston.

Racism and segregation must be rejected because they are contrary to human dignity and the founding principles of the nation. But are neighborhood schools like old South Boston High examples of "segregative intent," as Judge Garrity put it? It's worth remembering that *Brown v. Board* was an affirmation of the right of all children to attend school in their neighborhood. It did not forbid neighborhood schools.

December 12, 2008
Academy of the Pacific Rim, Hyde Park, Massachusetts

In 2000, the Boston Schools Committee finally dropped race as a factor used in student assignment. Today the city has a system of "controlled choice." Split into three zones, North, East and West, parents may apply to schools within the zone where they live. Boston also has several competitive exam schools, over a dozen public charter schools that are open to students living anywhere in the city, and 18 pilot schools, charter-like schools formed in collaboration with the district and the teacher's union.

Charter schools occupy something of a middle ground between busing and a strict system of neighborhood schools, and offer another route to empower parents and communities. Parents who want to send their children to a neighborhood school still have that option. But charter schools give parents options when their kids are ill-served by a local school.

I visited the Academy of the Pacific Rim, a charter school that combines the traditions of high quality East Asian education— standards, discipline and character education—with the strengths of the Western tradition—an emphasis on individual merit, personal creativity and societal diversity.

Fifty percent of the Academy's students are at or below the poverty line, but that isn't a bar to their goals, says Principal Jenne Colasacco. Like all public schools, the Academy is required to test 10th graders in Math and English by administering MCAS (the Massachusetts Comprehensive Assessment System). All of Pacific Rim's sophomores had passed the test on their first attempt, and their scores on average were well ahead of students in Boston and Massachusetts overall. Colasacco said MCAS scores prove that "students of color and poverty" can do as well as their more affluent peers.

Pacific Rim is located in Hyde Park, a working class neighborhood of longtime residents and recent immigrants on the outskirts of Boston. It is open to residents from across the city, but most of its 475 students live in Hyde Park or surrounding areas, including Dorchester, West Roxbury and Jamaica Plains. The school is located in an old warehouse next to railroad tracks. From the outside, it doesn't look like a school, but Principal Colasacco is not concerned. She knows buildings don't teach kids, and she has confidence in her top-notch staff.

In Boston, parents are clamoring for charter schools. In 2007, they submitted 5,649 applications for 1,249 open seats.

January 5, 2009
Greenwich and Bridgeport, Connecticut

"Byrdes of on kynde and color flok and flye allwayes together."— William Turner, *The Rescuing of Romish Fox*, 1545

Education on the "Gold Coast"

The suburbs near Long Island Sound in southwest Connecticut are called the "Gold Coast." The region, an hour north of New York City, is speckled with towns like Greenwich, New Canaan, Westport and Darien that are among the top 25 wealthiest in America. They are home to financial advisors, business consultants and lawyers who make up the country's professional upper class. I visited the area and spoke with several families about their lives and aspirations. Let's call them "Gold Coast family."

Gold Coast family is conflicted about its own wealth and elite status. It drives an expensive car, but an older model. Traditional wooden cutting boards—once a sign of organic awareness—are out; plastic ones—and hygienic bleach—are in. The family dog comes from a pound and is on anti-anxiety medication so that it can safely play fetch in the family great room—what the New York Times once called "the McMansion's signature space."

K-12 education is important to Gold Coast family. Its kids might attend one of several elite private schools, but—this surprised me—they are more likely to attend a top public school with other Gold Coast kids. Because of high property values and zoning restrictions, public schools like those in Greenwich resemble elite private schools in all but name. The families are proud of what little ethnic diversity does exist at their school and bemoan segregated schools elsewhere. Gold Coast parents frequently take the kids to museums and concerts in the City. At the dinner table, they talk about a visit to the French Embassy to obtain a special visa for Junior who will study in Paris.

A "good" college, the Holy Grail for Gold Coast teens, is something to plan for early. The pressure to "go Ivy" is intense, and it's thought that signs of community service will help guarantee admission. That's why it's important to volunteer at the animal shelter on Saturdays from 9:00-10:00 a.m. and to join the Recycling Club, which meets every other Thursday evening. A sterling college admissions letter is also essential. The family has purchased a copy of "Best College Admission Essays" and has consulted with a family friend who is an admissions officer to learn which essay themes are currently "in" and which are "overplayed." A tutor for SAT prep classes is necessary too. Of course, it's all a rat race but the game must be played: "How can one afford not too?"

Gold Coast families live near New York City for work but settle in Connecticut for the schools. Greenwich real estate companies advertise that Greenwich public schools are among the best in the nation. Greenwich High School has over 2700 students, one of the largest in the state, but it's divided into five houses, each with its own housemaster, guidance counselor and support services. The school offers over 300 courses and has a 97 percent graduation rate.

A Basketball Game: Greenwich High v. Bassick High

As part of my research—and because I love basketball—I attended a game between Greenwich High School and Bassick High School, which is located in Bridgeport, one of the poorest cities in Connecticut. A thirty minute drive separates the two schools. The Bassick neighborhood is one of frame houses and low-end apartment buildings, liquor stores and fast food restaurants. Graffiti mar the school's outer walls, although the school's inside is secure and well-maintained. I set off the metal detector on my way into the gym.

In contrast to Greenwich, Bassick's graduation rate hovers at around 60 percent, and for the past five years the school has failed to meet the "Adequate Yearly Progress" standard required by the No Child Left Behind act. Before the game in Bridgeport I spoke with a Harvard College admissions officer who was in town to interview applicants. Most Bridgeport applicants, she said, "are woefully under-prepared and would be absolutely swamped at Harvard." She sees 40-50 applicants each year, and says it's lucky for a single Bridgeport applicant to be accepted. The difference between Greenwich and Bridgeport, she says, "might be the widest disparity between neighboring districts just about anywhere."

Why the wide disparity between the two schools? Is Connecticut failing to correct a disparity in funding?

Public education is historically a local government function paid for by property taxes. This has meant that wealthy towns spent more on schools than poor towns, and that sometimes is still the case: Greenwich (#1 in town wealth) overall spends $17,000 per pupil, Bridgeport (165th in town wealth) about $12,000. But despite this sizable funding gap in community expenditures, the state of Connecticut has managed to even out much local area school spending. Divide the state into fifths, from richest to poorest, and it turns out that the richest quintile and the poorest spend almost exactly the same per pupil, about $11,000 (in 2003), both well above the national average.

But although spending gaps have been reduced, the achievement gap persists. The National Assessment of Educational Progress ("the nation's report card") reveals that the difference in scores between rich and poor students in Connecticut is the largest of any state in the nation. However, the cause is not a discrepancy in school funding; it's one of family income. Almost every student in Bassick High qualifies for free or reduced-price lunch compared to only seven percent of Greenwich students.

Unless the state of Connecticut makes it illegal for towns to raise local revenue to spend on local schools, there will always be some discrepancy in spending between towns. There's a trade-off between community control and funding inequities. Still, no matter how much the state spends to equalize school finance, major differences between districts and similarities within districts will remain. *Birds of a feather flock together.*

State governments can equalize school funding, but that won't mean the schools will be the same. Disparities in education will remain as long as there are vast differences in student backgrounds—students' lives outside of school. It takes much more than money to make a school.

January 9, 2009
Tolman High School, Pawtucket, Rhode Island

Tolman High School is located in the Rhode Island town of Pawtucket, which local boosters claim is the birthplace of the American Industrial Revolution. Slater Mill, the first successful cotton-spinning mill in the U.S., was built here in 1793. As I stood at the site of the historic mill I could see Tolman's cupola just upriver. I thought Tolman must be a converted mill building because it's a physically impressive structure rising four stories from the steep bank of the Blackstone River, once called "America's hardest working river." The Blackstone's banks are peppered with sprawling brick mills from Providence all the way to Worcester, Massachusetts. But, no, the banks of the Blackstone near the school were too steep for water-powered mill operations in the early nineteenth century. Tolman was built in 1926.

Although there is no connection between the construction of the mills and the school, the ties between industry and education in Pawtucket are close ones. Industrialization both spurred and hindered public education in early New England. Susan Boucher, in her *History of Pawtucket*, observes that the state expected public education to ameliorate the social effects of industrialization by alleviating urban poverty and helping to assimilate a burgeoning immigrant population. However, the state's interest in education was often in conflict with the mill owners, who depended on child labor, and with many parents, who looked to their children, some as young as age six, to supplement the family income. Pawtucket was founded in 1828, the year Rhode Island passed an act mandating public education. But school attendance was poor in those years even though the school year was only three months long.

Tolman High School was built during the last boom of the Pawtucket mills, and its size and grandeur—it featured an indoor pool and an auditorium holding 1440 students—reflected the community's prosperity. However, the onset of the Great Depression broke northern mill towns' monopoly on manufacturing, and Pawtucket and its public schools have not been the same since. After inspecting Tolman, a state education department visiting committee recently reported, "The major portion of the facility is in urgent need of attention," and concluded, "The stress that economic restraint has placed on the school is evident."

The school's physical condition is a reflection of Pawtucket's social and economic condition. Today, the issues facing Tolman are those confronting large urban public high schools across America. On an average day, 15% of Tolman's 1300 students, or 195 students, don't attend class (2002-03). The school's dropout rate was 39% (2004). Scanning through old news articles about the school, I read that 25 students were suspended for bringing weapons to school (1995); that there was a shooting at a school dance (1996); and a vicious beating that lead to the creation of a school violence committee (2002).

I wasn't able to schedule a formal visit, but I did get a more candid perspective from three students who were cutting class. One boy told me he was "supposed to be a junior" but had failed for two years and was still a freshman. Two girls sat on the steps of the church next door to the school, texting on their cell phones. They were skipping Spanish because it was presentations day. "The teacher won't know, or care. We'd get in trouble if we got caught, but we're not gonna get caught," they said. They disliked almost all their teachers and thought their feelings were returned. "They're just here because teaching is their job."

One girl commented on fights at the school: There were "more than a couple—a lot." Most were between freshman boys over "you talking sh*t." Of course freshmen fights in any high school are not uncommon. I attended a mid-sized rural public high school and remember a number of freshman fights within the first week of school. The tough atmosphere at Tolman, though, is also clearly a reflection of conditions in the surrounding community. After a beating at Tolman in 2002, Superintendent Dr. Hans W. Dellith wrote a letter to the *Pawtucket Times* explaining why his efforts to keep the schools safe had not succeeded: "Unfortunately, many of the problems in our schools are reflective of society as a whole."

To a great extent Dr. Dellith is correct. Students who come from broken homes in economically depressed communities can't leave their problems at home. Problems follow children to the schoolhouse door and into the classroom. When a school acquires a bad reputation it can't easily recruit and retain the best teachers. It's a cycle in which students like the ones I talked with inevitably skip class, fail, and drop out.

January 14, 2009
St. Benedict's Preparatory Academy, Newark, New Jersey

It was a frigid winter evening and I was visiting Newark, New Jersey to watch the Gray Bees of St. Benedict's Preparatory Academy, one of the best high school basketball teams in the country. Before

81

the game, my brother and I bided our time at the Springfield branch of the Newark Public Library in the city's central ward, a once Jewish neighborhood now almost exclusively African-American. The library is located five blocks east of Bergen Street, where the worst destruction occurred during the riots of 1967 which lasted six days and left 26 people dead. The area remains mired in poverty, crime and unemployment.

The library was small but warm. As my brother and I—white men with a laptop—sat playing a game of cards, two Hispanic girls wandered over to watch us play. Soon nearly all the kids in the library had gathered round our table, calling out cards and trying to figure out the game. One boy was soon calling out "A" and "J" for the aces and jacks.

Aside from the Hispanic sisters, the kids were African American. The boy who joined our game said he hung out at the library almost every day until closing time. He lived with his dad, but his mom and sister lived in Ohio. Like the other youngsters there, he was a library child with nowhere else to go. These elementary and middle school-aged kids were friendly and looking for attention, only beginning to hide the hurt under a veneer of toughness that would harden in high school.

The kids began talking about "hot" new horror movies in theaters, and flipped through a picture book about rappers. One boy let us know which rappers were "gang-bangers" and which were not. He wanted me to visit his school so I could learn about gangs.

"Who are the gangs?" I asked.

"It's the Latin Kings and all them, we've got a lot of Hispanics," he said, explaining that they start fights all the time. "Her friends," he continued, nodding toward one of the Hispanic girls. She knew one of them, he said, mentioning a name. The girl denied it, but agreed that fights were common, usually between black and Hispanic gangs.

The boy told me he'd been "jumped" at school, and "they said they were gonna do it again, so I had to defend myself, so I brought a knife to school." Although he did not use the knife, bringing it to school is grounds for expulsion from the school district, and he was expelled. He was 12 years old. The boy now goes to a correctional school "far away."

Kids join gangs to meet emotional needs, argues Harvard professor Deborah Prothrow-Stith. "Adolescence is a time of transition between the community of family of birth and the community of one's own family. Peer groups are vital. Research indicates that gang members tend to come from troubled, violence-ridden families. Since they often cannot get a sense of community from their families, their need for peer group community is even more acute." Looking at the lonely kids in the library that night, I could see how Prothrow-Stith came to her conclusion. As one New Jersey gang member put it: "We're not a gang, we're a family. We're a community."

Healthy families don't thrive on violence or rationalize their group aggression as community. But, says Prothrow-Stith: "Dysfunctional families, school failure, unemployment, poverty, and social dislocation all destroy a youth's sense of self esteem. What can they take pride in?" Family, even in the extreme, has been a source of intense pride. Think of the Montagues and Capulets "two households, both alike in dignity," feuding in Shakespeare's Romeo and Juliet, or the Hatfields and McCoys in the American backcountry—or the Sopranos of New Jersey. Gangs also build pride, cultivate loyalty to companions, and protect "turf."

The kids got rowdy as our conversation about education and gangs tapered off. The librarian broke in: "You don't laugh in the library—you remember that." The library was closing. I turned up my coat collar against the night as I headed for the door. On my way out the librarian caught my eye and whispered, "Be safe."

My brother and I walked to the unassuming gym at St. Benedict's, which gives no hint that this is one of the best high school basketball teams in the country. Warm-ups clear up any confusion; it's not often you see a team throw alley-oop dunks to every player, including the 5'9" point guard. St. Benedict's Prep is a perennial powerhouse in high school athletics and its reputation enables it to attract sports talent from around the world. Great players come to play with, and compete against, other great players. The basketball team has three players from Canada, and players from Cameroon, Latvia and Lithuania. They blew Curtis High School, from Staten Island, out of the game.

The players from across the globe coming to St. Benedict's want to be in a community with other outstanding players. But consider also the two Benedictine monks—dressed in black habits and scapulars—who sit in the stands near the team bench. The monks take the Benedictine vow of Stability of Place, the foremost of the three Benedictine vows. It is a vow of lifelong commitment to serve in a geographic place. It's been a pillar for the school, even as massive demographic shifts have changed the neighborhood.

The appeal of both types of community is powerful. One is chosen (as exemplified in the basketball team) while another embodies the monks' commitment to a place. As I look at schools across the country, I've concluded that parents select school communities to be with other parents who share their values and interests. However, powerful and longstanding ties to communities where individuals grew up or where they now live often hedge this bent towards chosen community. Picking a community isn't like picking a grocery store. It's more like planting an apple orchard. It takes time and the roots run deep. At some point, people make a stand. This is my town, this is my city, this is my school, and I'm going to work with that.

January 15, 2009
Lancaster, Pennsylvania

An hour west of Philadelphia is Lancaster County, Pennsylvania, the heart of Amish "Dutch" country. Amid picturesque small towns, farms and green rolling hills, over 50,000 Amish and related denominations live and work much as they have for three centuries. The Amish presence has made Lancaster County a major tourist attraction: 8.3 million visitors arrive here each year by bus and car. They come to take a peek at an older and simpler way of life, of horse and buggy, barn-raisings and one-room schoolhouses.

Amish are successors of 16th and 17th century European Anabaptists, a Reform Christian denomination. They immigrated to the United States to escape religious persecution, settling mainly in Pennsylvania and Ohio. Famous to the outside world for shunning many forms of technology, including cars, television and modern dress, the "Old Order" Amish model their lives after their 17th Century German predecessors. They emphasize the traditional family, simple work—farming and crafts—and devotion to God. They hold church services in German, speaking a form known as Pennsylvania Dutch (for Deutsch).

Their simple way of life extends to schooling. The Amish attend one-room schoolhouses, small white buildings that dot the Lancaster County countryside. Schools are kept small so children stay close to home, and almost all Amish schoolchildren walk to school. Formal schooling ends in 8th grade for the Amish, who believe excessive pursuit of worldly things, including formal education, distances them from God. They take literally Paul's warning to the Colossians: "Beware lest any man spoil you through philosophy and vain deceit after the rudiments of the world, and not after Christ."

The Amish effort to educate their children after their own manner and tradition met resistance early in the 20th century, a time when public officials adopted the ideas of progressivism and began to consolidate and enlarge local school districts. State governments and expansive school districts began to supplant local communities as the providers of education. They strengthened compulsory education laws and raised the age for mandatory school attendance.

Education was professionalized, and the professionals insisted they knew better than unenlightened local folk how to educate children. They viewed Amish schoolteachers, most of them young women and none with more than an 8th grade education, as unqualified, and were dismayed by the simple Amish schoolhouses with no electricity. But the biggest headache was the Amish practice of discontinuing formal education at 8th grade. It simply would not do.

The officials began to fine Amish parents whose children stopped attending school, and some fathers were jailed for refusing to send them to high school. To comply with the law the Amish began to make their children repeat 8th grade over and over until they reached the age at which they could stop going to school. Though the law enforcers were relentless, public opinion was with the Amish. Many non-Amish offered to pay the fines imposed on Amish parents.

In 1972, after decades of struggle, the Wisconsin Supreme Court appeared to settle the question of school attendance in favor of the Amish. In *Wisconsin v. Yoder* the court ruled that the benefits of universal education do not justify the violation of the Free Exercise Clause of the First Amendment. The U.S. Supreme Court agreed. The Amish could have their own schools and could educate their children in their own way.

I found a small book at an Amish bookstore that seemed to sum up the matter. According to the author of *A Little History of Our Parochial Schools and Steering Committee:* "It is the opinion of the writer and history has strongly proven that for the Amish it is much better and with more respect from the non-Amish and blessings from the higher powers, if they, in a humble and unified way cooperate as far as religiously possible, and if they can not cooperate with the general public or the world, then request no assistance from the outside world but, for example, in schools, build their own schools from their own funds and still assist in paying the public school taxes as before."

Mennonite schooling

In Lancaster I stayed with a very cordial couple in their late 20s who are Amish-Mennonite. Amish-Mennonites, they explained, split in the 19th century from the more traditional "Old Order Amish." They disagree with the Amish practice of shunning apostates, use modern technology and have adopted looser standards of dress.

Their lifestyle is a mix of old and new. Both the Amish and Amish-Mennonites tend to keep to themselves, but this couple lived in downtown Lancaster. He works on his family's five-generation old fruit farm, which produces apples, apple cider, apple butter and apple snitz (dried apple slices for baking and snacking), and has begun taking college courses online. She raises their child and runs a small daycare facility.

Their meals are simple and wholesome: fried scrapple and eggs—and cider—for breakfast, with homemade butter. A wood pellet stove heats the house. They drive a car but have no television. Both dressed conservatively. They don't make their clothes, as many Amish continue to do, but buy them from stores. The house has a computer and other modern conveniences. Theirs is a traditional household, but more similar than different from modern life.

They arranged for me to meet their friend, a Mennonite school-teacher. I visited with "Mr. Jones" in his perfectly ordinary 6th grade classroom after his students had left for the day. Twenty desks were lined up in rows; there was a blackboard and a corkboard to which were pinned magazine cutouts of current events. Aside from Bible class, the school subjects are typical of any grade school. The school uses Christian curriculum publishers and Mr. Jones' only complaint about the publishers was what he considered an overly militaristic tone in some of the social studies descriptions. Amish and Mennonites are pacifists.

Whether to go to high school is debated in the Mennonite community. Mr. Jones has a high school education, and he attended a five-week Mennonite teacher-training school. But only about half his students will go on to high school, and he was not defensive about this. Life experience, he argued, was the great teacher, even of teachers. "I've learned more from teaching than from any education I received," he said. He was humble about his own teaching ability (as he was about everything) and said Mennonites could use better-educated teachers and principals. But he recognized a trade-off: "I value education and I value community. I don't want to push education at the expense of community."

Higher education is costly in time and money. Jones said that if he wanted a college degree, he would have to leave his community for several years and incur a financial debt before returning to his life in rural Pennsylvania. He would need a higher wage to pay off his student loans. In so many words, Jones was saying that more education would price a Mennonite right out of the Mennonite way of life.

Jones' concern to put his community first was explicit. Teachers are fully integrated members of the Mennonite community and are expected to instruct students in the conduct of life as much as in the content of their lessons. Parents expect teachers to be role models. In terms of scripture, education is discipleship. First, children model their behavior after their parents at home and then after their classroom teachers. Jones said Mennonite K-8 education isn't remotely career-oriented or even learning-oriented as is modern public K-8 education because "We all know better." Education is about character development and becoming a better person. "I'm here to change my students, to change who they are as people."

Community members administer the school. The school board is comprised of five fathers, one of whom serves as principal. "Parents have a lot more say and influence here," said Jones. "The kids are respectful because they were brought up that way. If I have a problem, the parents are on my side." Possessing a common understanding of the ends of education builds a relationship of trust between parents and teachers.

"When there's a job to do, we all do it together," Jones said. This ethic applies in the classroom. Older students and those who are quick learners help the others. A very valuable part of Mennonite education, Jones said, is that "slow kids are right in the mix with everyone else. They may be intellectually disabled, but they have something to offer." There are no special education classes. "There is a place for each person God has put on this earth."

The Amish are atypical, but is their quest to control the direction of their children's education unique? The Amish struggle raises a larger question that transcends the peculiarities of the Amish: Who is responsible? Who ought to control the child's education? For the Amish, control begins with parents and extends to the small Amish community surrounding the child. The Amish have long resisted directives given from on high by those distant from Amish values and their way of life. They resist what Adam Smith, in *The Theory of Moral Sentiments*, called the "man of system," "who seems to imagine that he can arrange the different members of a great society with as much ease as the hand arranges the different pieces upon a chess-board. He does not consider that the pieces upon a chess-board have no other principle of motion besides that which the hand impresses upon them; but that in the great chess-board of human society, every single piece has a principle of motion of its own, altogether different from that which the legislature might choose to impress upon it."

January 16, 2009
Chester County & Chester Middle College High Schools,
Exton, Pennsylvania

Once I left the Amish and Mennonites of Lancaster, it was but a short drive back to the modern world. East of Lancaster I pulled into an office park in the Philadelphia exurb of Exton, where I met with Christopher Watson. Watson is the principal of two "alternative" public schools.

One is Chester County Middle College High School, whose long name belies its simple purpose: It is a high school located next to a college campus that gives its juniors and seniors an opportunity to take both college courses and high school classes at the same time. There are actually a fair number of "middle college high schools" around the country. They aren't meant for ambitious whiz kids seeking to get ahead, but for academically able students who have pulled away from high school routine. Many students, Watson told me, are dealing with anxiety and self-esteem issues caused by the social pressures of high school. At Middle College, they benefit from a smaller and more mature setting.

Watson's second school is Chester County High School, which is geared toward drop-outs and students at risk of dropping out: Think of it as "second chance high." Students enroll in one of two three-hour sessions, in the morning or afternoon. The truncated schedule provides more flexibility for the students, most of whom work or have families. Watson emphasized that although this is an alternative education program, no judge forces them to attend. Students choose to go, "which makes all the difference."

These "alt-ed" public schools cater to small subsets of the high school population. Watson oversees both specialty programs, which are run by the Chester County Intermediate Unit, rather than by an individual school district.

To understand how alternative public schools in Pennsylvania operate, Watson said I needed to know the role played by Intermediate Units (IU). IUs were created by the Pennsylvania legislature in 1970 to provide educational services that were too specialized for local school districts to handle effectively. They bridge the gap between a local school district and the state. Pennsylvania has 29 IUs that serve the state's 501 school districts.

IUs provide highly specialized services while reducing program duplication. Moreover, according to a 1997 report explaining their purpose, IUs spur the "development of school districts staffed by more competent persons" while preventing the "dissipation of professional energies." IUs, in other words, are another step in the ongoing professionalization and consolidation of Pennsylvania's public schools.

Because Pennsylvanians like local control of their schools, the IUs could hardly be justified solely by appealing to school administrators' interest in expertise and efficiency. So the report employed a moral argument that IUs "can further help advance the principal of equity." IUs would direct and concentrate services for poor school districts by drawing from a larger tax base than that available to local school districts.

Is a state obligated to promote "educational equity"? As I saw in South Dakota and Connecticut, that claim has been heatedly contested for several decades, driven by lawsuits and court rulings. At the time of the 1997 IU report, there were two lawsuits alleging that Pennsylvania's funding scheme was not "thorough and efficient."

The plaintiffs fought an uphill battle. In 1998 in *Marrero v. Commonwealth*, the Pennsylvania Supreme Court laid out in detail the reasons why a court was not the place to decide education funding.

The Court said: "More than forty years ago, this Court recognized that because educational philosophy and needs change constantly, the words "thorough and efficient" must not be narrowly construed." Furthermore, neither the legislature nor the court could "bind the hands" of subsequent legislators, and prevent them from modifying the education system as succeeding generations and changing times prescribe. The "rigid rule that each pupil must receive the same dollar expenditures" is not appropriate, because "expenditures are not the exclusive yardstick of educational quality, or even of educational quantity…"

I think Pennsylvania's court reached the right decision for the right reasons. During my school visits across America I've seen that there is no one path to a quality education, no one mold for what constitutes educational excellence, and no set price tag to achieve it. Local autonomy, independent control and parental choice give schools the incentives to tailor their programs to student needs. In the case of public schools, giving responsibility to local citizens and elected officials within a school district builds community involvement and support.

It makes sense that specialized schools like those run by Chris Watson should be run by a regional entity like the IUs. But ever-greater school centralization for the sake of funding equity creates a trade-off because local control is lost. That's a trade-off that should be decided by citizens of the state acting through their elected officials, not by courts.

* * *

February 20, 2009
Dollarway School District, Pine Bluff, Arkansas

Dollarway High looks just as it did before the school consolidation. It's at 4900 Dollarway Road, in Pine Bluff, Arkansas, a town of 55,000 south of Little Rock. Physically, it's a typical public school, tan-colored, low and sprawling—although the barbed wire fence around the campus is foreboding.

The school building hasn't changed, but the district has. In 2006 state policymakers merged neighboring Altheimer School District with the Dollarway district. To date, Arkansas has pared the number of its school districts down to 245 following a plan originally suggested by the Arkansas Policy Foundation. Proposed: "The General Assembly should enact legislation which restructures...Arkansas' existing 311 school districts into not more than 134 "administrative units" where an administrative unit is defined as "one superintendent and an associated superintendent's staff." The Foundation estimated that streamlining would save taxpayers $175 million over ten years.

Like the arguments for Intermediate Units in Pennsylvania, the Arkansas proposal noted that small school districts prevent economies of scale. Powerful testimony came from an Arkansas mother who wrote, "How long will parents in large school districts continue to let their children be penalized by allowing millions of tax dollars to flow into small, inefficient systems? We cannot solve our educational problems by simply pumping dollars into our present inefficient systems."

But there's another side to the story. Jay P. Greene, chair of the education reform program at the University of Arkansas in Fayetteville, is more skeptical of consolidation's benefits. He estimates that salary savings will be smaller than expected, and points out that student achievement tends to suffer in larger schools and school districts. "The benefits of smaller schools and school districts," he writes, "may be related to the tighter connection they have to their communities and the more competitive market provided by having more districts." Unlike the Arkansas mother, Greene doubts the benefits of consolidation.

Abolish Local School Districts?

School district consolidation began in the early 20th century, but as late as 1932 there were nearly 128,000 school districts. Over the next 40 years, however, that figure dropped to below 20,000. The U.S. now has about 15,000 districts.

Dartmouth College economist William Fischel writes that school district size is the result of a "long and contested history." Voters are torn "between economies of scale, which once warranted larger districts, and local-voter control, which is greatest in smaller districts." The leveling off of school district consolidation would seem to indicate that voters have struck a happy medium. Their school districts are large enough to be efficient, but small enough to be manageable.

While voters are torn, pundits tend to favor consolidation. In *Time* magazine Aspen Institute president Walter Isaacson called for national standards and characterized the current setup "incoherent" and "wacky." In a December 1, 2008 *Wall Street Journal* article, former IBM CEO Louis Gerstner Jr., chairman of the Teaching Commission and a 40-year veteran of the school reform movement, added his voice to the consolidation movement: "Let's abolish local school districts." After decades of reforms, "the system as a whole is still failing." We know "what to do," wrote Gerstner, who advised the next president to "abolish all local school districts, save 70 (50 states; 20 largest cities). Education Secretary Arne Duncan might have heard Gerstner's call. Duncan recently said: "If we accomplish one thing in the coming years, it should be to eliminate the extreme variation in standards across America."

I couldn't disagree more. Children, families, voters and communities derive real benefits from local control. When people disagree, forced uniformity creates lots of losers. The differentiation created by local control creates choices for families and citizens. Families decide what sort of school they want for their kids, and citizens decide on the policies they want for their schools and the amount they are willing to pay for them. Fischel argues that voters are acting rationally in wanting to keep school districts small and funding local. Experts or the courts may claim their system is more efficient, but citizens know they are giving up a lot when they sign away control.

Those who claim to have the answer—to know "what works" for all children and families and schools across the country—find the current system "unwieldy." But unwieldy is just a word for saying that power is too dispersed for one person to tell everyone else what to do. Count me a supporter of unwieldy.

CHAPTER FIVE

Southern Comfort
January 24 – February 20

Reading lesson at a charter school in New Orleans

Some very thorny issues about governance and authority came up during this leg of the trip. In Raleigh, North Carolina, I spoke with unhappy parents about their school district's plan to bus to each others' schools high-achieving students from wealthier families and low-performing students from poorer families. The goal was to achieve an "appropriate and reasonable" balance of kids. The Raleigh busing program to integrate students by social class was about as popular as busing in Boston to integrate students by race. (The school board reversed the decision in March 2010 by a narrow 5-4 vote.) I also encountered unhappy students in Charleston, South Carolina who were protesting decisions by their local school board.

When it comes to special education, an increasingly popular alternative to having school bureaucrats make education decisions is education vouchers. The idea that public money should follow the child is working in Georgia and Florida where I visited private special education schools that make use of publicly-funded vouchers. I've also inserted into the narrative an account of my visit to a special ed school in Montgomery County, Maryland.

Vouchers for special needs students have proven attractive to voters. However, public support for general statewide school voucher programs weak. Why is that? I offer some reflections, and comment on a recent U.S. Supreme Court decision that underscores the contentious character of public funding for private education. The Court's split decision did not break down along the usual liberal-conservative divide, which suggests that old political categories don't always apply to these questions.

In Mobile, Alabama, I tried to learn more about single-sex public schools, and I was reminded that average Americans are unlike federal education officials and social science experts. They want schools in which kids learn, but they think learning is not the same as the kind of "academic achievement" that can be standardized and measured. I shared this feeling as I watched committed school reformers and energetic young teachers re-imagine education in New Orleans. Their ambitions and determination are impressive, but I question whether their plans for the city's schools after Hurricane Katrina can succeed without community support. Education reformers champion rigorous testing and evaluation and longer school days and school years, but these are no substitute for parents who love, encourage and reprimand their children.

You can argue that these goals are not opposed to each other, but I sensed the dichotomy in Mississippi where earnest Teach for America volunteers recite the credo of educational opportunity but mothers carry paddles to keep their children in line. Likewise, in Oklahoma I visited two schools: One was a "high-performance" KIPP Academy that promotes academic achievement by publicly posting its students' test scores. The other was a homeschooling cooperative that deemphasizes testing and accepts that children have different innate abilities and dispositions that need to be nurtured and cultivated.

January 24, 2009
Research Triangle, North Carolina

What is a "community school" and what's the alternative to it? In Wake County, North Carolina, this question is much on peoples' minds. Wake County is the heart of what is known as North Carolina's Research Triangle. The name comes from the three major research universities— Duke, the University of North Carolina, and NC State—in or near the cities of Durham, Chapel Hill and Raleigh, the state capital. An educated workforce has attracted high tech companies like IBM and Merck to the fast-growing region, and Wake County's public school system recently passed San Diego as the 18th largest in the country.

On a Saturday morning, I visited a first grade classroom in a public elementary school in a rapidly growing western Wake County suburb. About a third of Wake's schools, including the one I visited, have switched to a year-round calendar to accommodate the expanding student population. Students take periodic short breaks instead of a long summer vacation. When some students are in class, others are on break, so school buildings are in constant use. A snowstorm had closed school the week before my visit, and since there is no room for make-up days at the end of the year, the school was holding classes on Saturday.

"Just put your driver's license in the machine," the school secretary told me when I entered the lobby. The machine is a fancy device that scans a visitor's license and prints out a temporary ID badge with my name and picture. I affixed my sticker and walked to the classroom.

The kids were at first graders' tasks: reading books, coloring pictures, finding rhyming words. I sat next to a boy of South Asian background who was reading a book about pirates. That he liked pirates wasn't unusual, but I was surprised when he started talking in detail about the Somali pirates he had heard about on the evening news.

This school was located in a cluster of residential homes, and what homes they were—enormous and bewilderingly alike. I drove along roads with names like "Majestic Meadow Drive" and "Pleasant Run Road" that end at cul-de-sacs of well-manicured lawns in front of McMansions. The first grade teacher referred to the community with a touch of irony as a "little suburban paradise." But she was also in earnest. So much of school quality has to do with the demographics of the surrounding community. "Don't think I teach in a 'good' school just because it is a 'good' school," the teacher told me in a moment of candor.

During this trip I've learned that deciding where a child goes to school is the thorniest issue in public education. Most Americans believe neighborhood-based public schools are or ought to be the norm for education. They think public schools should be in a geographic neighborhood to serve children whose parents live nearby and pay property taxes for local public schools. The concept seems tried-and-true, particularly in small towns and rural areas.

However, a problem arises in large suburbs and cities where the issue of "student assignment" is caught up in policy debates that have become very complicated. There may be several schools variously located a reasonable distance from a child's home, and that leads to questions about whether it is always and obviously best to assign a student to a school closest to home. What about parental choice, community control, socio-economic balance and racial integration? Everyone has an opinion about how much weight to assign to each of these factors in determining the child's "best interest."

In Wake County, the Board of Education designed a plan to answer that question. Three goals are supposed to be met in making student assignments: making efficient use of school facilities, providing options for parents, and "assigning appropriate and reasonably diverse student populations to all schools." As for what is appropriate and reasonable, the Board's goal is that "individual schools reflect a free and reduced lunch ratio no greater than 40% of its student population and an achievement level of less than 25% of students below grade level." In other words, schools should be socio-economically integrated, with a mix of high and low-achieving students. The district says it uses family wealth, reading scores and growth trends—but not race or ethnicity—as "diversity indicators."

To achieve the goal of a student "balance," the district buses high-achieving students from wealthier families and low-performing students from poorer families to each others' schools. The logic behind busing goes back to the 1966 Coleman Report (officially titled "Equality of Educational Opportunity"), a survey of over 600,000 students and teachers. One of its most influential findings was that *"…it appears that a pupil's achievement is strongly related to the educational background and aspirations of the other students in the school."* Once policymakers were persuaded that a student's success in school was affected by his or her classmates, they endorsed busing to achieve racial and economic integration.

In Wake County fewer than ten percent of students are bused for diversity reasons, but the assignments can change from year to year, which has the potential to disrupt settled family expectations. It's an understatement to say that this makes many parents very unhappy. A recent assignment plan for Wake County reassigned almost 25,000 students to different schools over the next three years. The district's effort to "level the playing field" has raised the tempers of parents who have a different standard of what is "appropriate and reasonable." They feel families have a right to send their children to public schools near their homes.

I went to dinner with four teachers in the area who talked about their experiences. They observed that some parents in Wake have started homeschooling their kids because they're unhappy with the assignment plan. A rash of action-oriented groups and Political Action Committees have sprung up in Wake County, dedicated to electing school board members who will reform Wake County's assignment policy.

One group, Take Wake Schools Back, says the district needs to use "common sense approaches to assigning students to schools, rather than social engineering." Their #1 core value is "community schools" by which they mean: "Use of busing only to ease overcrowding as a short-term solution, while new schools are built in the neighborhoods that need them now." Another group called Wake Cares complained that the assignment plan was a ploy to make the district look good: "By taking low-performing students from a lower-performing school and placing them in a higher-performing school, fewer schools appear to be failing the children," said co-founder Kathleen Brennan.

Yet another organization, the Wake Schools Community Alliance (WSCA) supports "a community-based school system," but leaves obscure the definition of "community" and its relationship to parental choice and neighborhood location. The group's website says: "We believe community-based assignment should be inclusive as part of a parent's choice in education, not restricted by percentages. A community should be a stable resource that families can connect with, lean on when they need help, contribute to and help evolve. A community might or might not be made up of immediate neighbors, but are a set of people that children can grow to know and rely on for help over time."

North Carolina's second largest school district, Charlotte-Mecklenburg, offers a costly alternative to Raleigh's system. Rather than bus students to reduce socio-economic segregation, Charlotte directs millions of extra dollars to improve high-poverty schools. The *Raleigh Observer* compared Wake County's busing policy to the Charlotte-Mecklenburg approach and found little difference between the scores of minority and poor students in both districts.

However, Charlotte-Mecklenburg's policy is what Dana Cope, founder of the Children's Political Action Committee, would like to see for Wake County schools. "Let's focus appropriate resources on the low-performing schools," Cope said. "I'm sure that many parents at Lacy (the school his sons attend) won't agree with me, but Lacy doesn't need as many resources as we get from the school system, because we have a private foundation. Those resources should be reallocated to the low-performing schools in the school system."

Cope is angered that his two sons were reassigned to an elementary school to help reduce its percentage of low-income students. "How dare they use my children for a social experiment that has gone wrong and needs replacing," he said. "This is about transferring high-performing children to lower-performing schools to mask the performance of those schools. It's ludicrous."

The reason why parents are outraged by busing, whether for racial integration in Boston or socio-economic integration in Wake County, is clear to me. It's a matter of parental authority. Parents feel they've lost authority when a school district overrides what they consider their freedom to select a neighborhood to complement the home that shelters their children. This sense of powerlessness and lost authority is undermining the conditions that make possible support for public schools.

January 26, 2009
Oysters and Protests in Charleston, South Carolina

From a distance I could see the entire Arthur Ravenel Bridge stretching across the Cooper River as it flows past Charleston. The bridge's cables fanned out from two concrete towers, supporting an eight-lane highway in a high-tension balancing act, a web of steel support designed to withstand hurricanes and earthquakes. But the early morning fog hid the cables from view as I drove across the bridge, giving me the impression that it was floating over the water. I was on my way to Georgia, but stopped in the city after I had taken a detour to an oyster festival at an old cotton plantation.

On this particular Monday, the Charleston County School District Board met in district administrative offices at 75 Calhoun Street. About two dozen demonstrating students gathered outside holding protest signs. An older girl, the apparent leader, led the call-and-answer:

"What do we want?" **"Orchestra!"** "When do we want it?" **"Now!"**

The students' parents, also holding signs, stood on a building balcony behind their children. "S.O.S. - Save Our Strings" was their message. Reporters from two local news stations were nearby and an occasional passing car honked in support.

I asked the girl leading the chants to tell me what was happening. The school board, she said, was about to eliminate the string orchestra program at her school. Members of the orchestra and their parents were trying to stop that. The CCSD Board's position was that the proposed program cut was part of a structural change forced on the district by the "new fiscal reality." The district is facing a $28 million deficit for 2009-2010.

Should the string orchestra be saved? Which school programs merit public funding in a slumping economy? Tough choices bring citizens out in force. The Charleston board pointed out that during its redesign planning stages, "public engagement and community participation were at all-time highs."

I don't know if Charleston should keep the strings program, not that it's any business of mine. The decision is a local one, and different local constituencies—from taxpayers to orchestra members—should have the opportunity to plead their case. At the local level, self-government and citizen participation is the way things get done.

Parents and citizens believe they have a voice over education decisions made by local school boards, which is why they and their children were out in force. When decisions are made by state boards of education the parents' voice is diminished and when decisions are made by state legislatures or Congress, parents' only power is to cast a vote during an election. Political decisions are made amidst the buzzing hive of social scientists, bureaucrats and self-proclaimed experts who manage the affairs of the people. That's a trend Alexis de Tocqueville worried about in *Democracy in America*: "If one must conduct small affairs in which simple good sense can suffice, they [and by "they" Tocqueville meant politicians and their entourage of political elites] determine that citizens are incapable of it; if it is a question of the government of the whole state, they entrust immense prerogatives in these citizens; they make them alternatively the playthings of the sovereign and its masters, more than kings and less than men."

January 29, 2009
Chatham Academy, Savannah, Georgia

I've noticed trees in this part of the South are quite unlike those in New England. Outside Charleston, they line the long driveway to the plantation where I joined a crowd at an oyster festival. Similar ones flanked the streets in Savannah, towering with spreading branches draped in moss. In New England, the trees grow up not out. New England trees strive; southern ones endure.

In Savannah, I met with Carolyn Hannaford, principal of Chatham Academy. Chatham is a private school for students with learning differences. Entering students, who undergo a battery of psycho-educational tests, typically enter Chatham for learning differences such as ADHD (Attention Deficit and Hyperactivity Disorder) and LD (Learning Disability). Hannaford said the school had just seven students at its opening in 1978, but the number has grown to 100 students who are served by a staff of about twenty.

Many Chatham students are what Hannaford calls "system-abused." While she is quick to say the students' parents and the teachers at their prior schools were not "at fault," she says there was a need for something different than a regular school setting. Hannaford observes, "One of the first things that's bred out of kids who don't do well in school is that they quit being risk-takers." They stop raising their hands in class, or they listen to class instructions but give up without even trying to work through an assignment. Chatham is trying to remedy that by giving entering students a "honeymoon period" to build trust with their teachers and the school: think of the strategy therapist Robin Williams used with Matt Damon in the movie *Good Will Hunting*. The key for the school is to establish trust, then gradually increase the academic workload. It's a game of "push and pull," challenging but not daunting to the student.

Chatham's high tuition—about $13,000 a year—limits enrollment. Still, about one-quarter of the school's 100 students receive financial aid, primarily through a two year-old state voucher program. Senate Bill 10, the Georgia Special Needs Scholarship Act, went into effect for the 2007-2008 school year. Designed to "provide scholarships for public school students with disabilities to attend other public or private schools," it is a voucher program for special needs students. Hannaford is a fan. Chatham works hard to remain independent by not taking state or federal money, and the good thing about the scholarships is that they come with few heavy-handed restrictions.

Public school students qualify for a scholarship if they have "special needs," which in bureaucratic terms means that the school has devised an Individualized Education Plan (IEP) for them. The IEP makes students eligible to attend a public school outside their residence-based school assignment or even outside the school district if space allows. Students use their voucher to help cover the cost of an approved private school. To be approved, a private school must be fiscally sound, abide by all anti-discrimination statutes, health and safety codes, and employ qualified teachers.

Hannaford knows many private schools in the South "were started for the wrong reasons"—to avoid court-ordered desegregation: "Many of them are now closing," she said. She is proud that parents started Chatham for the right reason: to serve students who weren't receiving adequate services in public school. The school's mission hasn't changed in 30 years.

February 4, 2009
Solid Rock Community School, New Port Richey, Florida

My brother's New Year's resolution was to give up soda, but he's constantly looking for ways around this bothersome self-imposed restraint. He asked me to define "soda": Does it have to be sweet and bubbly? How about diet soda? Tonic water? What about Coke that's gone flat?

During my school visits I've discovered that defining a "public school" isn't easy or straightforward either. I used to define a public school as government-run and tuition-free, open to all and subject to government regulations and requirements. But some private schools are tuition-free (through vouchers), state regulated and admit all students, while some public schools are not government-run (charter schools) and can be very selective in the students they admit (Boston Latin). Outside Tampa, Florida, at Solid Rock Community School, I saw just how muddled the definition of a "public school" can be.

Solid Rock serves fewer than 100 students in grades 1-12, and occupies a large single-story facility. It is a non-profit private school with yearly tuition of about $9,000. But the school also accepts McKay Scholarships, a state government voucher program that provides public dollars so special needs students can go to non-government schools. During the 2007-2008 school year nearly 10,000 special needs students got vouchers—averaging $7,300—to attend private schools. Only a minority of Solid Rock's students had McKay Scholarships, but I had to wonder what if most or all of them had a voucher? Would that make Solid Rock a public school?

The Solid Rock students who take advantage of the McKay scholarships have learning disabilities. But other Solid Rock students are academically advanced and some just don't fit in a traditional classroom. Classes are based on skill levels—a concept that school director Michele Fasnacht carried over from her experience as a homeschooling mother. "We will not put a 9th grade 14 year-old in algebra just because traditional schools do. The student must show mastery of all math levels through pre-algebra to take algebra." I observed a math class where the age range was from 9 to 18. Fasnacht said skill level-based learning allows the school to accommodate both slow and gifted kids and handle those who do well in some subjects and poorly in others.

Fasnacht is a big supporter of the McKay Scholarship program and the theory behind it. "Public money should be tied to the child," she told me. If America switched over to that model, as other countries have, she said "it would change everything." Florida's McKay program, like those in Milwaukee and Cleveland, is an experiment along the margins of the idea, but Chile, Sweden, Belgium, the Netherlands and France, and to a lesser degree New Zealand and Great Britain offer instructive examples of what happens in programs where "money follows the child."

In 1989 New Zealand abolished residential school zones and set up open enrollments for public schools. The government also partially subsidizes private schools, providing 25 to 40 percent of state per-pupil expenditures, and gives nearly full state funding to "integrated" schools, an intermediary school similar to charter schools. This model corresponds to the "money follows the child" voucher system that Fasnacht favors. If Florida were to adopt this system the state would need to abolish its school districts, establish a system of open-enrollment charter schools, and partially subsidize private schools through tuition vouchers like McKay—a tall order.

Kathy Wylie of the New Zealand Council for Educational Research conducted a survey of vouchers and quasi-vouchers around the world. She is more cautious than Fasnacht in predicting the effect of vouchers because she sees a strong correlation between student demographics and school achievement. In summary she argues:

- Demography is central. A school's academic achievements are shaped by its students' natural abilities and the homes and communities from which they come.

- Student characteristics are largely formed outside and independent of school.

- Struggling students perform better if they attend school with succeeding students.

- School achievement is pretty much a zero-sum game: When one school "wins" by attracting good students, another school "loses" as those students leave.

Wylie notes that the biggest beneficiaries of school choice are high-ability, low-income students. They are the students most likely to use vouchers to leave poorly performing public schools and become high achievers in rigorous private or charter schools. I have to agree on the basis of what I've seen at "high performing" open-enrollment charter schools.

However, Wylie concludes that voucher programs are detrimental to education overall. She criticizes the "self-regard" that she says vouchers inculcate in families, increasing social stratification by student ability and background. From what I've seen, social stratification occurs whenever families exercise choice—but that includes choosing where to live so that your kids can attend a particular school. Wylie may be right that voucher systems increase self-regard, motivating the most success-oriented parents and students. But self-regard is a powerful and dynamic force for social improvement. Parents' "regard" for their children's success is not a lamentable quality—at least not in America.

Wylie bemoans the absence of a more equitable socio-economic mix in schools, which "is the most efficient way to reduce disparities and raise overall standards." But she admits that a mix won't be achieved "without deliberate intervention." I've seen how parents and communities react to deliberate intervention in Boston and Raleigh. Forced busing hasn't worked. Nor has turning education into a numbers game in which bureaucrats try to "balance" classrooms with an "appropriate" mix of students.

Voucher supporters believe giving parents direct control over the public money that follows their child is the best policy. But there is a powerful counter-argument: A voucher system takes choice away from community residents who think their tax dollars should stay close to home funding local schools that educate their children and their neighbors' children. That counter-argument is also based on "self-regard," and it is prevalent among suburban voters who have surprised voucher supporters by rejecting statewide school choice ballot initiatives.

Special education voucher programs like Florida's McKay Scholarships are more targeted and hence less controversial. That may be why they are the fastest growing voucher programs in the country. Providing vouchers only to special needs students skirts the thorny issue of stratification (i.e. the "creaming" argument that vouchers empower the best and most motivated families). It only minimally affects the majority of students and doesn't disturb the demographic makeup of public schools. Moreover, special education has always been largely a state and federal issue, rather than a local one.

The McKay program appears to be working. A Manhattan Institute study found that parents using McKay scholarships are more satisfied with their child's new school, and the private schools accepting the scholarships are more accountable. Another Manhattan study found that the voucher program did not harm special needs students who remained in public school.

* * *

May 13, 2009
Montgomery County, Maryland

In Montgomery County, Maryland, I visited Ms. Jones, a teacher who works one-on-one or with small groups of students with special needs at a local public elementary school. Even in this plush suburb of the nation's capital many kids need extra help. One of Jones's students is Sarah, a third grader who reads at the kindergarten level and has trouble paying attention for even short periods of time. Sarah is a special education student who receives extra help from Jones at the back of a regular classroom. I worked with Jones on Sarah's spelling lesson.

Sarah is in good hands, but what if her parents didn't agree? State law often allows special education students to attend a private school, and provides that parents will be reimbursed by the public school district for the private tuition they pay. Montgomery County is one of the country's wealthiest areas and it has comprehensive special education programs. Even so, last year county taxpayers paid the private school tuition of 614 special education students. The *Washington Post* reports that tuition costs "have risen from $21 million in fiscal 2000 to a projected $39 million in fiscal 2010." That's less than some neighboring districts. "Prince George's County schools, with fewer services, this year spent $56 million on 1,168 students. And the District, with a historically troubled special-education department, has 2,300 students receiving private care at a cost of $141 million." The students are frequently adolescent males who need more adult supervision.

The systems in Maryland and DC are like the special education voucher programs I saw in Georgia and Florida with one exception. In Maryland and DC the reimbursement for private school tuition is negotiated, and the negotiations are contentious. Parents often resort to suing the local school district to recover their tuition costs. The *Washington Post* reports that District of Columbia schools allocated a whopping $7.5 million of this year's $783 million school budget for prospective legal costs.

That may change thanks to a recent U.S. Supreme Court ruling, *Forest Grove School District v. T.A.* The case commenced when the 9th circuit court of appeals ruled that an Oregon school district must pay for the private schooling of a special needs child. The school district appealed the case to the Supreme Court. The issue concerned whether students with disabilities must first apply to attend a public school before they are reimbursed for private school costs. Parents questioned why they would be required to waste precious time sending their children to a public school that they already knew was unable to meet their needs. The lower court's ruling simply delayed receipt of the voucher that would pay for a private school's specialized education program.

But that wasn't the view of Nancy Reder, deputy executive director of the National Association of State Directors of Special Education. She argues that preemptively issued vouchers "open the door for parents to completely bypass the public school system and go directly to private school, and then ask for reimbursement."

In a 6-3 decision written by Justice John Paul Stevens, with the agreement of Chief Justice John Roberts and Justices Kennedy, Ginsberg, Breyer and Alito, the court ruled that parents may be reimbursed even though their kids have not received initial public school services. The majority concluded that since Congress requires public schools to provide a "free adequate public education," Congress did not intend for parents to accept inadequate public-school education while they waited for their lawsuit to be adjudicated.

The dissent was written by Justice David Souter, with support from Justices Antonin Scalia and Clarence Thomas. They argued that the law clearly required parents to try public schools first. "When a mother tells a boy that he may go out and play after his homework is done," wrote Souter, "he knows what she means." Likewise, "So does anyone who reads the authorization of a reimbursement order in the case of 'a child with a disability, who previously received special education and related services under the authority of a public agency.' If the mother did not mean that the homework had to be done, why did she mention it at all, and if Congress did not mean to restrict reimbursement authority by reference to previous receipt of services, why did it even raise the subject?" Citing the expensive nature of special education, the dissenters said it makes "good sense to require parents to try to devise a satisfactory alternative within the public schools, by taking part in the collaborative process of developing an IEP that is the *'modus operandi'* of the IDEA [Individuals with Disabilities Education Act]."

The question at issue in *Forest Grove* pertains to voucher programs in general. If a neighborhood public school "fails" children, shouldn't parents be able to send them to a different school? That's the logic behind the public school transfer polices that the No Child Left Behind law prompted states to adopt. It's also the logic behind publicly-funded vouchers. But voters in Utah and California have rejected comprehensive statewide voucher plans for understandable reasons (See Chapter 6).

Special needs students present a complicated case. Compensating parents for private school tuition, through vouchers or reimbursement, makes sense. But it also makes sense to require parents to try public schools first in order to control cost-shifting of private tuition onto taxpayers. Who decides whether reimbursing parents of special needs kids puts too much of a burden on the parents or the taxpayer? Because public money is at stake, community control is inevitable.

February 7, 2009
Hankins Middle School, Theodore, Alabama

Hankins Middle School isn't an unusual small town public school. It's in Theodore, Alabama, which is just outside the Mobile city limits along the Gulf Coast. Yet at the start of the 2008-2009 school year, Hankins decided to switch to single-sex classes, joining a handful of other public schools in the Mobile county school district. Boys and girls would now take English, math and the rest of their subjects apart from one another.

I assumed the school made the switch to boost academic performance and keep students from dropping out. The Mobile Area Education Foundation recently released a study of Mobile County's class of 2006, and its findings showed a disheartening number of drop-outs, mostly boys. The response? The American Civil Liberties Union (ACLU), which opposes gender-separation, threatened to sue the school district.

I was interested in the public's reaction to the decision and the lawsuit. I wasn't able to speak with anyone at the school, so I decided to talk to townspeople at the local downtown Piggly Wiggly grocery store. They threw me a curve ball. Of nearly 20 people I spoke with, not a single one had heard of the school's decision. Not until I talked to two high school kids (one with a younger brother in the middle school) was I able to confirm that the school had indeed switched to single-sex classes.

While no one knew about the Hankins' decision, most everyone had an opinion about single-gender classes. And while none seemed to care about whether single-gender classes help students learn, all had thoughts about their social and moral significance. I quickly realized that street corner sentiment is indifferent to the academic merit of single-gender classes.

A middle-aged black man said gender separation seemed too much like racial segregation. "They need to think twice, that don't make sense at all," he said of the decision. "I'm black, and I wouldn't want my kids going to an all-black school." But a woman liked the idea. "I hadn't heard of it, but I think it's a good idea. That way, no teenage pregnancies," she said.

The next woman was adamantly opposed. "I think it's stupid. It's human nature" for boys and girls to be together. She didn't like gender separation, but had deeper worries. "It's a problem that starts at home. If the parents would teach them morals, it wouldn't be an issue." Another woman also blamed the mores of society. "It's television's problem." A man was concerned that "you wouldn't know how to treat a girl" if the sexes were separated. An old black man was very candid: "I don't know, I never went to school." One woman said boys and girls should be together, and winked at her husband. Another thought they should be kept apart, and cast a mocking glance at her husband. Both broke out laughing.

I think it's great when parents have schooling options—single-sex or co-ed. As education blogger Joanne Jacobs put it, "The solution seems simple: Let parents choose single-sex or co-ed classes for their children and study the results."

Yes, definitely study the results. But my experience in Theodore showed me that when Americans weigh a school's decision, they are concerned with more than "the results." Sure, they may want to know how a decision may marginally nudge student test scores forward. But schools for them are more than factories whose sole purpose is academic.

The other "purposes" of schooling are, or ought to be, a contentious matter. There are competing academic, social, financial, political and religious values. Which deserves emphasis? What should weigh more: Preventing teenage pregnancy or keeping restless boys from dropping out? I've seen as many different answers to the question as the number of schools I've visited during this project. The answers vary from person to person, community to community and state to state. It's not a question with a right answer.

When most education researchers think about policy options, they almost always use some form of "academic achievement" as their measuring stick for what constitutes good policy. Perhaps this value is at the top of their list because they enjoy academic social science research or because test scores are quantitative and tests can be standardized. That makes it easy to compare and contrast schools and policies. But beyond the world of the policy wonks, academic achievement is only one of many competing values that parents and communities cherish. It's their values that usually are, and ought to be, reflected in our schools.

Hankins abandoned single-sex classes in March 2009, less than a single school year after implementing them.

New Orleans' public schools have projected an image of failure for a long time. According to national tests, the scores for the city's students are in the basement. As Paul Tough wrote in a 2008 *New York Times Sunday Magazine* article, "In New Orleans, before the storm, the schools weren't succeeding even in an incremental way. In 2005, Louisiana's public schools ranked anywhere from 43rd to 46th in the federal government's various state-by-state rankings of student achievement, and the schools in Orleans Parish, which encompasses the city of New Orleans, ranked 67th out of the 68 parishes in the state." No one was surprised by news stories of graduating high school seniors who are unable to read.

The Orleans Parish School Board (OPSB) is responsible for educating 65,000 students in the city's 127 schools. But in 2003, Louisiana legislators gave the state the power to take over poorly performing schools from OPSB. The state-run Recovery School District initially took control over five of the worst schools. Then, on August 29, 2005, Hurricane Katrina crashed onto the Gulf Coast. When the New Orleans levees burst, many of the city's schools were literally washed away and many of those left had few or no students. The storm forced officials to make some radical and long-overdue changes.

It was a gloomy Tuesday when I drove over Lake Pontchartrain and into the Big Easy. It was Mardi Gras month and the beginning of festivities was only days away, but the city didn't have a festive feeling. As I drove through the neighborhoods I saw vestiges of storm damage. Many houses were torn down, and although some lots were rebuilt others were empty. My host pointed out the high water mark lines of discoloration on the sides of houses, and I saw the fresh concrete poured where sections of the levee were breached. I also saw school buildings, destroyed and abandoned.

Education reformers, however, saw an unexpected opportunity. Coming into the city from across the country, they wanted to be a part of the rebuilding process. Many are young and idealistic charter school advocates and Teach for America workers excited to use New Orleans to make a "statement" about urban education: If schools can teach the kids of New Orleans, they can teach kids anywhere.

A system of schools, not a school system

At the center of the energetic effort to remake the city's education system is an organization called New Schools for New Orleans (NSNO). A nonprofit founded after Katrina, NSNO's strategy is to "build a system of schools, not a school system." The strategy is essentially one of decentralization. Rather than have a single organization like the Recovery School District (RSD) take over and run all city public schools, NSNO would have the schools contract out their operations to a host of different education providers, under RSD supervision.

Supporters of decentralization, such as NSNO, argue that the technique provides the "autonomy and critical accountability structure" necessary to improve schools. Says Louisiana state education superintendent Paul Pastorek, "Over the long haul the R.S.D. becomes an instrument that evaluates existing schools, supports existing schools, recommends the closure of schools and recommends the best operator to come in and take over, or the best operator to come in in place of that school. We put people in business, and we take people out of business."

NSNO is launching and supporting the charter schools that make up the new "system of schools." It reports having set up 9% (seven schools) of all current city public schools as well as providing funding to 20% and governance services to 43%. It also helps recruit and train the teachers and school leaders the new schools require. A third leg of its work is explaining the new system to the community, and providing parents with information about school options.

That third task will become more important over time. The old system had the advantage of relative simplicity. But the "system of schools" approach introduces dozens of providers and several oversight organizations jostling for position, working in cooperation and competition. Both the RSD and the OPSB run their own schools, as well as oversee independent charter schools. In addition, there are magnet schools, selective admission schools, open-enrollment schools and neighborhood schools. Some are considered top notch, others are schools of last resort. "The State of Public Education in New Orleans," a 2008 report prepared by Tulane University, identified eighty public schools that were run by 29 different operators.

I had the opportunity to visit three of the new NSNO charter schools: Akili Academy (Swahili for "wisdom"), Langston Hughes Academy, and Sci Academy. From the outside the schools look similar. All are housed in temporary buildings. Like many schools in the city, they are a cluster of mobile homes connected by gravel pathways and corrugated stainless roofs.

They serve different grades: Akili Academy is limited to grades K-1, but plans eventually to expand to 8th grade; Langston Hughes is for elementary and middle school students; and Sci Academy serves ninth graders with plans to become a four-year high school. All have a similar feel inside and out: They fit the model of high performance, college-preparatory charter schools. Students dress in uniform and test score improvement is priority number one. In a trailer back room that is Akili's administrative office I encountered an entire wall plastered with charts, numbers and student names. It gave the reading and math scores for children in kindergarten and first grade along with formulas and timetables to track their progress. The school's expectations for its five and six year olds are ambitious.

The schools have increased the length of the school day and school year to mark their goal of sending all students to college. Langston Hughes reports that its students will spend 50% more time in school than peers in a traditional public school. In addition, teachers are expected to be on call. "Parents and students will be given a directory with the cell phone number for each of their teachers. Teachers will accept calls until 8pm nightly to assist with homework and bridge the link between home and school."

Ben Marcowitz, a school leader at Sci Academy, told me his students learned little in their old schools as they advanced from grade to grade. Expectations were low, and there was little classroom structure or rigor. The words hit home when I walked into the remedial reading class at Sci. I saw three 9th graders, two guys and a girl, sitting at a table with their reading coach. They were reading, barely, at a first grade level. It was sobering to watch teenagers struggle to read "The cat jumped into the box." I worried that my presence would embarrass the students, but if they minded, they didn't show it.

More than any other city New Orleans has a unique opportunity to recreate a structure of public education. In a difficult situation, it's off to a promising start. The "system of schools" model has energized city leaders to organize many different schools. It gives opportunities to innovative and diverse organizations and attracts bright and optimistic people to New Orleans to work in education. In a social studies class at Sci Academy I watched as a teacher called on his students. He expected thoughtful answers from each of them, and prodded and coaxed until he got it. He was stern, but his students seemed engaged and attempted to meet his high expectations.

Is Testing and Evaluation the Answer?

As soon as the kinks are worked out for the new, decentralized approach to running New Orleans' public schools I believe it will prove more effective in responding to the needs of families and students. However, I was skeptical that the New Orleans charter schools I visited can sustain themselves. The teachers exhibited a fever pitch of intensity that will be hard to maintain for more than a few years, and I question whether their practices can be replicated for schools across the country.

Almost all the New Orleans charter school staffers are young and unmarried, without families. Most came from Teach for America or other alternative recruiting programs. As I listened to their conversation, I realized they had created a specialized network. They are very familiar with other "high-performing" charter schools across the country—they know who runs them and who works in them. Principals take pains to grab the most talented teachers away from other schools, and this tends to create hiring patterns that are "win-lose." There are only so many Ivy League whiz kids who want to work 18-hour days in inner-city schools.

The teachers and principals coming to post-Katrina New Orleans are members of what I call the Blackberry Gang. They like to say their decisions are "data-driven"; they refer to "recruiting talent" rather than to hiring a teacher; and they imagine that they are applying a business/networking model to education. They put in incredibly long hours and make themselves available to their students at all hours of the day and night, weekdays and weekends, school year and summer.

Many openly say they are trying to be a child's family. It's hard to fault their good intentions, but as I looked at the reams of test scores they assembled and posted on the back wall of Akili Academy, I knew this was a bad idea. Five year-olds are not objects for evaluation moving along an assembly line, all to be fitted out with the same bits of added value that can be quantified and measured. That's not how education works. Educators cannot hope to succeed by expecting evaluation and testing to substitute for parents who encourage and reprimand their kids, and educational services cannot compensate for the absence of meaningful ties between children and their families and communities. The more teachers try to do that, the less they will accomplish.

Rick Hess, an education scholar at the American Enterprise Institute, describes the danger of giving too much importance to education data: At the end of the day, "educators should be wary of allowing data or research to substitute for good judgment." Teaching kids isn't the same as making Big Macs or shipping FedEx packages.

Sean Gallagher, the leader of Akili Academy, hinted as much when he described how he would like to move his school into a permanent building and settle into the community where most of his students live.

He recognized that something intangible but powerful was created by placing a school within a student's community. Reformers talk about open-enrollment schools, charter schools and voucher programs that break down residential-based student assignments, creating conditions for school competition and improvement. On this trip I've tried to highlight these programs and innovative schools responding to parental choice. But going to school close to home is as natural as bread and butter for a small child, and most parents simply want their child in a quality, *neighborhood* school. That's a reality reformers must take into account while working to improve the way our education system is structured.

Sci Academy's Ben Marcowitz told me his school was a stopgap at best: if it was successful at fixing the problems he observed, it would put itself out of business. Marcowitz looked forward to a time when there wouldn't be a need for as much of his school's intensity, rigidity and structure, as well as the extended school day and year and the three hours of math and English each day. I agree with Marcowitz that the Academy's structure is too intense to sustain for long. Moreover, if the underlying problem is a breakdown in families and communities, then more time in school is not the answer. Comprehensive schooling, however well intended, could be harmful.

Consider the comments of John Gatto, who was a New York State public school teacher of the year:

"A surprising number of otherwise sensible people find it hard to see why the scope and reach of our formal schooling networks should not be increased (by extending the school day or year, for instance) in order to provide an economical solution to the problems posed by the decay of the American family. One reason for their preference, I think, is that they have trouble understanding the real difference between communities and networks, or even the difference between families and networks.

"Because of this confusion they conclude that replacing a bad network with a good one is the right way to go. Since I disagree so strongly with the fundamental premise that networks are workable substitutes for families, and because from anybody's point of view a lot more school is going to cost a lot more money, I thought I'd tell you why, from a school teacher's perspective, we shouldn't be thinking of more school, but less."

Gatto's analysis cuts to the heart of the issue: "Schools are already a major cause of weak families and weak communities. They separate parents and children from vital interaction with each other's lives." Expanding the sphere of formal schooling in an attempt to reverse complex family and community problems won't work.

In his article about the new look of New Orleans' schools, Paul Tough quotes education historian Diane Ravitch: "The fundamental issue in American education—I say this after 40 years of having read and studied and written about the problems—is one that is demographic." Demographics aren't limited to blunt measurements of race socio-economic status, but include the myriad relationships, expectations, values and support of family and community.

During a remedial English class at Sci Academy I observed teenagers who couldn't read and was told that their old schools had failed them. I wanted to cry out: "No, it's bigger than that!" School may have failed these kids, but where were their mothers and fathers? Where were their aunts and uncles? Where were their basketball coaches and pastors? Where are the family and community? It's a bigger issue than school failure. Unless we realize that, our improvement efforts will not only fail, they will be counterproductive.

February 20, 2009
Leland, Mississippi

All the country stations were playing Brad Paisley's #1 hit, "Start a Band" during my drive across the Florida panhandle and then north through Mississippi. The song begins:

I never was a straight-lace, straight A student, teacher's pet or child prodigy.

The song is about kicking back and enjoying the simple things in life, and I'm sure a pundit somewhere even now is criticizing the song for celebrating underachievers. The song was coming in loud and clear on Cat Country 98.7 out of Pensacola, and sailing out the open car windows into the warm winter air as I pulled into a Boy Scout camp in southern Mississippi. The woman running the camp told me it was for Boy Scouts only, but upon hearing our story, she opened up and agreed to put us up for the night. "Just close the gate when you leave, and don't tell anyone you were here," she said. So my brother and I spent the night in one of the little canvas tents, which was uneventful but for the mouse that woke my brother up by running across his face.

Driving along the Mississippi River the next day, past Vicksburg and up the Delta, was like taking a journey back in time. The area is farm country and poor. Trailers and tiny houses dot the countryside, amid small cotton patches, peanut farms and orchards. Brush is often being burnt in front of the trailers and the kids ride around on four-wheelers. When I stopped at a gas station, I watched as several truckloads of

112

farmers and kids pulled in to pick up a drink for the ride home. There were two 55-gallon drums full of ice, one for soda and the other for beer sold by the can. The weather was hot, even in early March. The grocery store in Leland, Mississippi, hometown to Muppet creator Jim Henson, was stocked with the basics and not much else. It was as far from a Whole Foods market as can be.

In Leland I stayed with several first-year teachers from the group Teach for America (TFA). Quite isolated from area residents, they stayed close to one another. They had joined TFA for different reasons—some wanted to see the country and learn about different cultures, others wanted experience with a nonprofit or aspired to close the achievement gap. None were interested in becoming career teachers.

They explained that their students' "zip-code"—meaning where they're from as well as their race, socioeconomic status, background and culture—should not determine their education. That is a Teach for America credo and it sounds good in theory, promising a blank slate and uniform educational opportunity for all. The problem is that children, even the youngest, aren't blank slates, and they aren't educated in a vacuum. Schools rarely have the power to overcome culture, and as a general rule I don't think we want them to. Children's educational experiences should be rooted in their families and the places where they live.

I visited a TFA teacher's 4th grade classroom in Indianola, one town over from Leland. All his students were black, and they insisted that their teacher and I must be brothers because we were both white. As class photos were being taken, the teacher told me a story that illustrated how much culture trickles into the classroom. It seems a fellow teacher had brought a student to the office for misbehaving. The boy's mother was called, and the principal offered her the school paddle, which was kept in the office, to spank her son. The mother said no. Instead, she took her own paddle out of her bag and gave her son a couple of solid whacks "until the snot and tears were flying."

Paddling, or corporal punishment, is lawful in 21 states, and remains a common form of punishment in several. The Mississippi Education code states, "corporal punishment," which means the reasonable use of physical force or physical contact, may be used as necessary "to maintain discipline, to enforce a school rule, for self-protection or for the protection of other students from disruptive students." Mississippi reports the highest rate of paddling, at 7.5% of students paddled in 2006-2007. It's overwhelmingly boys who catch the paddle.

Proverbs 13:24 says, "He who spareth the rod hateth his son: but he that loveth him correcteth him betimes." Through iterations in literature and popular culture we have "spare the rod, spoil the child." To many people spanking in public schools is barbaric and out of date. But as one Mississippi woman commented on a website about the subject, "spanking is very much a visible and shared part of our culture in the South." Those who won't spank are suspect.

The Jackson Free Press newspaper reports that 98 of Mississippi's 152 districts allow for the use of corporal punishment. Because each Mississippi school district makes its own decision whether or not to allow corporal punishment, I suppose Mississippi families and taxpayers have some choice over how public schools treat their children. If you don't support paddling, you can vote with your feet and move to a district that doesn't allow it, taking your children and tax dollars with you.

Education vouchers are a less troubling and more direct way to empower parents to pick schools that align with their values. This is the approach economist Milton Friedman recommended in a 1955 article, "The Role of Government in Education," which subsequently appeared in his book *Capitalism and Freedom* (1962). Of course, vouchers provided by government limit the control non-parents have over where their education tax dollars are spent. This raises the question: To what extent should decisions over public education be reserved for parents, and how much should be exercised by representatives of the taxpaying community?

Consider a recent *New York Times* report on the diverse neighborhood of East Ramapo, New York. The area has a large, wealthy, Orthodox Jewish community, but it is predominantly African-American and Hispanic. While most of the Jewish families send their kids to private Jewish schools, Orthodox Jews also are a majority on the public school board in East Ramapo. Burdened by the weight of high public school taxes and private school tuition, they recently decided to close one of the district schools. Some residents are "chafing at the idea that people who don't send their children to the public schools are making the decisions for those from very different cultures who do." Nathan Rothschild, president of the East Ramapo board, has a different point of view: "I take great offense to the idea that you can tell a specific part of the community, 'You're not entitled to run for office.' That's outrageous."

Giving local residents other than parents a say in the spending and policy decisions of local public schools makes sense if you expect them to pay for public education. Even as he promoted education vouchers Milton Friedman understood the importance of community control. In his essay he wrote: "What forms of education have the greatest social advantage and how much of the community's limited resources should be spent on them *are questions to be decided by the judgment of the community* expressed through its accepted political channels [emphasis mine]." Friedman recognized the fine line between empowering parents and disenfranchising other residents.

February 20, 2009
Soulsville Charter School, Memphis, Tennessee

Elvis, Johnny Cash, Muddy Waters, Robert Johnson, B.B. King, Al Green—they were all born or raised in Memphis and northern Mississippi. Many were connected with Stax Records, a record label based in the Soulsville neighborhood of Memphis, the heart of the soul music industry in the late 1960s and early 1970s. Stax Records went under in 1975, but its old building is now home to the Soulsville Charter School.

The school is run by NeShante Brown, a down-to-earth former Memphis public school teacher who aims to ground learning in the area's musical and cultural heritage. To demonstrate the "interconnectedness of music and academics," all her students participate in the Soulsville Symphony Orchestra, and devote 90 minutes each day to music education.

While neighborhood schools serve neighborhood children, charter schools must serve "high priority" children (Tennessee law requires that Soulsville Charter must serve struggling students in failing schools or students from low-income families). Memphis also runs about three dozen Optional Schools, which are a major part of the city's "public school choice" plan. Most are special programs that operate within traditional schools. Similar to magnet schools in other cities, option schools began in the 1970s as part of the district's plans for school desegregation.

The schools have specific themes—college preparatory, fine arts, Montessori, technology—but their main difference is the entry requirement. Consider Overton High School, whose open house I attended. The school's website indicates that its students must score at or above the 50th percentile on the English and Math portions of the Tennessee achievement exam as well as successfully complete an interview or audition. Those admitted to the program must maintain a 2.0 GPA every semester, pass all their classes, and have satisfactory attendance.

"When you have a choice in selecting your children's school," said Linda Sklar, director of Memphis optional schools, "you have a lot more ownership in it." Parents consider all sorts of factors when they decide on a school, but a very important one is the other families who will be sending kids to the school. Sklar continues: "And I think that parents like having their children with other students whose parents have high expectations."

Sklar's observation cuts to the heart of one of the truest and trickiest components of the "school choice" debate: the choices parents make are heavily contingent on the choices made by other parents. When deciding which school is best for their child, they consider who their child's classmates will be. One reason why Option Schools are popular in Memphis is the school communities they create. Families with similar educational expectations bond together over their children's educations. That only happens because the schools can select whom they will admit. In a roundabout way, when parents choose an option school they are approving the school's right to exclude other parents' children.

February 24 and 28, 2009
KIPP Delta Prep, Helena, Arkansas &
Cornerstone Tutorial Center, Tulsa, Oklahoma

KIPP (Knowledge is Power Program) operates dozens of charter schools around the country, schools that have become the poster child for high-performing, college-preparatory charter schools. Most are in urban areas, but the one I visited, Delta Prep, is one of only a few KIPP schools in impoverished rural areas. The tiny town of Helena, on the Arkansas-Mississippi state line, has the feel of a place that's hanging on but has seen brighter days.

Delta Prep educates students in fifth through eighth grades and is housed in a converted train depot. As a pair of student "ambassadors," a boy and girl in 8th grade, gave me a tour of their school I noticed that in the hall next to every classroom were bulletin boards. They listed student names and posted test scores next to them. It's unusual for a school to be so public with this information, but KIPP believes the public display of progress spurs students to work harder. "There is a lot of pressure from the school to do well on tests," both students agreed. The girl pointed out her scores and admitted that she was struggling, but said, "I'm not embarrassed."

To prepare for the tests, Delta Prep devotes extra class time to math and English. Its other practices and policies are common to charter schools: longer school days and a longer school year, student uniforms and school-wide discipline policies, young non-unionized staff and a cohesive culture focused on sending all students to college. My student guides recognized that Delta prep was a challenging place and told me that friends in their old school thought of KIPP as "torture." But they didn't see it that way. They attributed their own enlarged ambitions to the school's high expectations.

KIPP Delta Prep gives families in Helena a choice to accept more rigor and pressure, longer hours and higher academic expectations. It is succeeding as its students post impressive results on core subject tests. Opponents counter that charter schools post high test scores because they draw ("cream") the brightest or most motivated students away from traditional public schools, and there is some truth to that. My student guide explained that several of her friends started at KIPP but lasted only a couple days before deciding to return to the town's public school.

Rudolph Howard, superintendent of the school district, has a different take on the matter. He says a small town like Helena can't support two public schools, warning "One is going to die, one way or another, particularly in small areas like this one, where every student provides the revenue to support quality programs." The man may feel his back is up against the wall, but I think more than naked self-interest is involved. KIPP is well-known to education philanthropists around the country, and KIPP Delta Prep is looking to them to support its ongoing capital campaign to build a gymnasium. It's expensive to open and operate a school. A small town may be no more able to support two schools and two administrative staffs than it can support two grocery stores or movie theaters.

What would happen if Delta Prep put the Helena public school out of business? It might be a good thing to have KIPP the only game in town. That's the benefit of competition. But KIPP would then be serving all the town's students, including those who drop out because they think school is "torture." They might change KIPP more than KIPP changed them.

Cornerstone Tutorial Center: Deemphasizing Testing

I'd been on the road for nearly seven months when I left hot, dusty Helena and drove northwest across Arkansas and into northeastern Oklahoma. In the town of Broken Arrow, near Tulsa, I made my way to the third floor of a large white Baptist Church. There Susan Strelow runs a homeschool "school" called the Cornerstone Tutorial Center (CTC). As the organization's website describes the school, "CTC is like a college for home schooled students. Families pick and choose the subjects they want their students to take here at CTC. Classes meet one or two days a week. Parents then supervise work that needs to be completed on the other days of the week."

Strelow founded CTC as a support program for area Christian homeschooling families. Parents volunteer to teach classes, and students come together once or twice a week in an arrangement known as a homeschool cooperative. The cooperative model is common for homeschoolers, particularly those who keep their children home beyond grade school. Over the years CTC has grown more formal and structured; it has a board of directors and now hires teachers. Parents pay by the class, and write a check directly to the teacher/tutor, who works on contract with CTC. Currently there are about 100 students.

Unlike KIPP, CTC deemphasizes testing and there is no public display of scores and rankings. Strelow said most CTC students wouldn't know their "grade level." For Strelow and the parents who choose CTC, that's an attractive feature.

Most of the parents I heard from at CTC say homeschooling makes formalized testing unnecessary. Because they know their children better than anyone, and work with them individually, they are in tune with their child's academic progress. I spoke with a class of students who all said they enjoyed CTC and the social interaction it provides. One boy blasted the No Child Left Behind Act as "dumbing everything down to the lowest common denominator," and several other students agreed.

Mostly they were anxious to disprove the stereotype of Christian homeschoolers. "We don't live in a holy box," they said. "We're not ignorant." One boy turned to his friend and joked, "What's at the center of an atom, John?" The boy replied, "God and Jesus." Then he quipped back, "What's the force that pulls things down to earth?" "Faith!" The class started laughing, and I thought it was a pretty clever joke. They informed me their routine was from a "Saturday Night Live" skit.

Is KIPP right to emphasize testing and public posting of test scores? Or is Cornerstone right not to? There is more than one way to skin a cat. My brothers and I were homeschooled in elementary school and my parents did a first-rate job. When we moved to Iowa, the four of us had to take the Iowa Test of Basic Skills. We all scored differently. The variance was due to our different innate abilities and dispositions, which my parents were well aware of. The test was no reflection on the job my parents had done raising and teaching their kids.

Statewide testing and uniform national standards didn't come about because they are more effective than parents and communities at assessing children's and schools' performance. They are what modern schooling systems require, providing benefits and efficiencies wherever school districts are large and bureaucratic and local communities are mobile and transient. By contrast, homeschooling requires lots of personal time and attention from families. It requires a parent who stays at home.

Testing and standards may be poor substitutes for the old methods of accountability, which worked where families and communities were more stable and ties more intimate. But school accountability, as in so many other areas, is preceded and shaped by society, whose structure and culture are changing.

Swinging through the Sunshine States
February 24 – April 1

Driving to Odessa, Texas

It's February and I am fortunate to be traveling through the Southwest to California and Hawaii. Sitting in the booth at a Whataburger restaurant outside Dallas, I listened to a mother describe her frustrations at the impact increased student enrollments at her daughter's school are having on her child's education. The woman's dilemma suggested that kids and their families can change schools more than schools change them, and raised what were now familiar problems concerning school assignment and parental choice .

In West Texas I visited Odessa, the town whose high school football stadium was made famous by the book *Friday Night Lights*, which later became a popular film and TV series. On to Phoenix, where I looked into Arizona's innovative education tax credit program to help low-income families pay private school tuition for their children. The question of "community" vs. "parental" control of taxpayer education dollars keeps popping up on this trip, and it surfaced again in California and Utah, two states where voters have decisively rejected statewide voucher programs. Even though vouchers aim to give parents more choice in schooling, many affluent suburbanites vote against them, fearing their effect on their own local schools and communities.

This leg of the trip also took me through Las Vegas, where vocational-technical education has been transformed, and Honolulu, where the state's unique education model is attracting attention around the country.

In the fall when I called home from places like Fargo or Omaha my friends and family in New England would sometimes confess they were worried about me. But it seems anxiety has given way to envy when I call from Las Vegas and Honolulu in the middle of winter.

February 26, 2009
DeSoto District, Dallas, Texas

For three generations members of Jill Robinson's family have taken pride in graduating from DeSoto High School, the only public high school in this Dallas suburb. But changes at the high school have caused the Robinsons to consider selling their house and moving away so their daughter can attend a different school. As we sit in a booth at the town's Whataburger restaurant, Mrs. Robinson explains the reasons for her frustration.

Desoto has been forced to absorb many students from nearby Hutchins, a school district that the state closed several years ago for financial mismanagement and poor academic performance. Along with the Hutchins influx, there are Hurricane Katrina refugees and increasing numbers of students from Hispanic immigrant families. Mrs. Robinson suspects many parents don't live in DeSoto, but lie about their address or just drop off their kids at the bus stop. "No one is held accountable."

Robinson senses an erosion of standards and discipline, and she has watched as good teachers flee in droves. "People have deserted ship." Robinson doesn't want to be one of them, but feels she has exhausted her options. In part, she blames the school board. It allows anyone in the high school to take AP (advanced placement) courses—no entry exam is required—and students can't be dropped for failing. Robinson's husband ran unsuccessfully for a spot on the school board.

Robinson decided it was time to act when DeSoto High recently received a rating of "Academically Unsuccessful" based on student scores on the state exam. At first she tried to transfer her daughter to a neighboring public school using Texas's Public Education Grant (PEG) program. Robinson broadened her search after her daughter's PEG transfer application was turned down. Deterred by the cost of private schooling, the family looked into a nearby charter school, but rejected it because it had no music program—their daughter plays the French horn. Next they applied to Booker T. Washington Magnet School in Dallas, an elite and very selective public school in the city's downtown. "If she doesn't get accepted [at Booker T. Washington] we're considering putting the house on the market," Mrs. Robinson told me. "We feel like we're being forced into moving and we don't want to move."

The Public Education Grant (PEG) progam

In theory, the PEG program sounds perfect for the Robinsons. In DeSoto, students are required to attend school in a designated attendance zone and transfers are usually approved only in cases of bullying, sexual assault, and the like. However, the PEG option comes into play when poor student test scores cause a drop in a school's performance rating.

The PEG transfer option specifies, "An eligible student may attend a public school in the district in which the student resides or may use a public education grant to attend any other district chosen by the student's parent." Under the PEG program a student is eligible if his school is rated academically unacceptable in any of the three previous years. Students may only transfer to a higher performing school.

The option isn't unique to Texas; several states promote it as a school choice element in their "testing and accountability" programs, which are similar to the federal No Child Left Behind (NCLB) law. These programs were implemented both before and after enactment of the federal law. They are supposed to be a win-win proposition: Parents get a school upgrade and low-performing schools get tough love, a combination of pressure and incentives to spur school improvement—in theory.

The catch is that the decision isn't really in the hands of parents. The code continues, "A school district chosen by a student's parent…is entitled to accept or reject the application for the student to attend school in that district." So the school districts have the final say on whether to accept a student transfer application. The district cannot discriminate on the basis of athletic or academic ability or socio-economic status, but it must give preference to students at risk of dropping out. In other words, districts are pressured to accept only the most difficult students.

Predictably, very few schools accept transfers. As one article explains: "The majority of school districts don't accept transfers through the PEG program, even if they have empty seats. In 2001 more than 141,000 Texas students were eligible to transfer to a better school, but fewer than 200 students did."

Are Vouchers the Answer?

If the PEG program won't give families like the Robinsons better schooling options, what will? Some Texas school reformers take the idea of PEG a step further and have proposed school vouchers: Let public money follow the child to whatever public or private school a family chooses.

The Children's Educational Opportunity (CEO) foundation tested the voucher idea in one Texas school district. In 1998, the CEO foundation sponsored and funded a voucher program for the Edgewood school district, just west of downtown San Antonio. I drove through the district, whose most notable feature is a sprawling cemetery lined with palm trees. From an overpass, I looked down onto railroad tracks and a scrap yard. Restaurants advertise the enchilada platter in this low-income Hispanic community. I saw homemade signs advertising houses for "50 cents on the dollar!" and read about local property tax revenues so meager that over 80% of the area's education funding comes from the state and federal governments.

CEO dubbed its voucher experiment the Horizon Program and committed $5 million a year for 10 years to pay school tuition to help low-income parents send their kids to any public or private school in the Edgewood district. Nearly every child in the area qualified for the program. There was a public relations angle to the privately-funded experiment: If privately-funded Horizon "worked," so might publicly-funded voucher programs.

A 1999 study of Horizon's first year impact found that voucher and non-voucher families had similar incomes. No surprise there, since the district was homogeneous and the vouchers were available to all students. There was some indication that certain kinds of parents were more likely to use vouchers. For instance, children whose mothers were working full time and had more schooling were more apt to participate in the voucher program. Voucher-using parents reported more satisfaction with their child's school and felt it was safer. But researchers found after one year that voucher participation had a minimal effect on student test scores. The Horizon program's ten-year anniversary is this year and researchers will be eagerly awaiting evaluations of it.

Whatever the outcomes, I suspect the results of the Horizon voucher program—whether it is judged a "success" or a "failure"—will not be decisive for other communities. Vouchers have upsides—they promote competition among schools and appear to satisfy parents and make schools more responsive to them. But they are not a cure-all for education woes, nor will they make Mrs. Robinson's decision any easier.

Why not? Mrs. Robinson and her family were happy with their local public school for several generations. That's because the families who lived in DeSoto and sent their kids to the local high school had similar values and expectations for their children. When the neighborhood changed, the school became unacceptable to the Robinsons, who could do nothing to make the school reflect their past expectations.

Education by and large is a communal activity that generates differences of opinion. A school's internal structure and dynamics—its academic standards, codes of conduct, and curricular offerings—are determined in great measure by its students and their families, no matter whether the school is public or private. Education experts argue that teachers, teacher unions, local school board politics, and state and federal education policies all influence the make-up of a local school. But as I've traveled across the country visiting schools and talking to parents and students, teachers and administrators, I am persuaded that the real character of a school is the result of its students and their parents. And this is as it should be.

I've also concluded that the most important question for parents is *who else* is in their child's school. On this trip the biggest and most surprising lesson I've learned is that parents want a measure of control over the identity of their child's *classmates*. They want their child's classmates' parents to have the same values and expectations for their children as they have.

How is this possible? In a country where public schools predominate and students are assigned to the schools closest to home, parents get to exercise this control indirectly by choosing their place of residence. They seek out comparable communities of families, and then send their children to the local public school, which reserves its seats for neighborhood kids.

Proponents of school vouchers aim to increase parental control directly over education. But unless voucher schools are allowed to pick and choose their students—through entry exams or something similar—vouchers aren't likely to give Mrs. Robinson the option she wants. That's because the issue isn't whether the school is public or private, or in her neighborhood or far away. What counts is the student composition within the school.

Because Mrs. Robinson was dissatisfied with her local public school she was prepared to look into the PEG program, which has voucher-like features. But parents who are satisfied with their neighborhood school worry that vouchers may make things worse for their kids. They are concerned that once everyone has vouchers, neighborhood schools won't hold places just for neighborhood kids. The concept of a neighborhood school will be lost if everyone with a voucher has a right to send their children to any school. Is this fear overblown? Does it disguise suburbanite race or class bias? These are issues I explored in California and Utah where I looked into the states' failure to enact school voucher ballot initiatives.

What about "Equalizing" School Funding?

Some reformers claim the best way to fix schools is to equalize funding among them. If more state and federal funds went to improve poorly-funded schools, then families like the Robinsons wouldn't need to move, they say.

The state of Texas has already taken momentous and controversial steps to equalize education funding. Consider the Edgewood school district. Besides the CEO voucher experiment, Edgewood was at the center of a series of funding-equity lawsuits that culminated in 1989 when the Texas Supreme Court ruled that students in Edgewood and other property-poor districts were victims of discrimination. What came to be known as "Robin Hood solutions" were undertaken to force more equalized spending between school districts. Neighborhoods filled with expensive homes that yield high property tax revenues were required to finance education spending in school districts where homes were inexpensive and incomes were low.

The goal of Chapter 41 of the Texas Education Code—the "Equalized Wealth Level" provision—is to restrict the amount of money a wealthy district can spend on education relative to other districts. To level the playing field, a wealthy district is required to pair up with a poor district, or educate students from a poor district, or turn over its "extra" money to the state for redistribution. Hence the name "Robin Hood." Will equal school funding fix what ails a school district that lacks quality schools? Money counts, but I doubt it will accomplish what reformers expect. What do families look for in selecting a school?

To explore this issue further, I spoke with a professional with an intimate and detailed knowledge about what families want—a real estate agent.

Real Estate and Schools in Dallas

Parents and homeowners are well aware that the quality of an area's local schools has a substantial effect on real estate values. It's been 20 years since the Texas Supreme Court mandated that public school spending be more or less consistent among all districts. What's been the effect of the mandate to equalize school funding? If it has improved area education, won't that be reflected in real estate prices?

I spoke with Arlene Beckerman, a real estate agent who has lived in the area for 31 years. In her opinion the relationship between school districts and real estate prices is as strong as ever. She showed me the brochures on DFW (Dallas/ Ft. Worth) area public schools that she gives prospective homebuyers. They are based on the TAKS (Texas Assessment of Knowledge and Schools) state test, and they report on the academic ranking—from "recognized" to "unacceptable"—of all area school districts.

The agent explained that the Dallas area is split by the Trinity River into North Dallas and South Dallas. Residents progress up the ladder in home values and school quality by moving from the southwest, to the south, to the north. "South of Trinity, families either try to have their kids in a private school or a charter school," she said. By the time you get to North Dallas, "public schools are really like private schools." The school district remains a major selling point when buyers go house-hunting. Beckerman had just spoken with a client interested in purchasing a home on the border of two districts, Mansfield and Grand Prairie. The client was adamant that she wanted to be in Mansfield, not Grand Prairie, where she wouldn't consider buying a house. The difference in location was only twenty feet, but that twenty feet made all the difference. Twenty years after the state Supreme Court mandated school funding equalization, Grand Prairie receives about the same amount of funding as Mansfield. But that hasn't convinced parents and homeowners that the school districts are comparable.

I went for a drive to give school buildings in the DeSoto District the once-over and compare them to schools in the surrounding districts of Cedar Hill and Lancaster, areas with lower property values. The difference wasn't in the school buildings. Parents choose one school over another because of the educational environment created by the families that make up the school community.

In the beginning, there was oil. A town took shape as the oil was drawn out of the West Texas desert, and with the ensuing oil booms and busts the town's fortunes rose and fell. But the town always had something to rely on—high school football season. Every fall Odessa, Texas, faced the tantalizing prospect of the boys, our boys, taking state.

I arrived in Odessa in the middle of a hot afternoon, after leaving San Antonio and driving for hours across hundreds of miles of endless expanse. Odessa, with a population of 90,000, is home to the headquarters of Family Dollar stores, the University of Texas of the Permian Basin, and two public high schools, Odessa and Permian. Permian High School—its mascot is the Panthers and its nickname is MOJO—was the high school whose football team is chronicled by H.G. Bissinger in his book *Friday Night Lights*.

I went straight to Ratliff Stadium, where the Panthers and the Odessa Broncos play. Built in 1982 for $5.6 million, it is one of the grandest high school stadiums in the country. It has a sunken playing field and seating for 19,000, though on game nights as many as 23,000 people squeeze in. The green field is an oasis amid the brown tumbleweed and sand stretching for miles in every direction, a monotonous landscape disrupted only by the gentle swinging movement of oil pumps.

Odessa high schools may be known for their football teams, but they recently attracted attention for a different reason. The two high schools in the Ector County school district were the subject of a 2007 lawsuit brought by the ACLU that challenged the elective Bible classes both schools offered in their curriculum.

In 2007 a bill encouraging public schools to offer an elective academic course on the Bible sailed through the Texas House and Senate and was signed into law by Governor Rick Perry. The purpose of the Bible classes, according to the bill, was to "teach students knowledge of biblical content, characters, poetry, and narratives that are prerequisites to understanding contemporary society and culture, including literature, art, music, mores, oratory, and public policy."

Just days after the bill passed, the ACLU filed suit against the Odessa school district challenging its elective Bible courses. The challenge was brought on behalf of eight families with students in school, though none attended the Bible courses. In March 2008, the case was settled. Odessa kept the courses but was required to modify the curriculum, which had been developed by the National Council on Bible Curriculum in Public Schools. Both sides claimed victory. About

40 students in the two public high schools are now enrolled in the Bible course.

The U.S. Supreme Court has decided that the Constitution permits public schools to teach about the Bible in a secular education program, and the number of school districts offering Bible classes is on the upswing. Time Magazine ran a story in 2007, "The Case for Teaching the Bible," reporting a Bible curriculum in some 460 districts in at least 37 states. The numbers are modest, but Bible curriculum publishers say demand from public school districts is on the rise.

As I stood on the rim of Ratliff Stadium and looked down on the field, and then out to a church in the distance and an oil rig beyond it, I recalled a passage from Bissinger's *Friday Night Lights*. The author recounted what had happened to several of the football players ten years after their glory days. Brian had gone on to college in Boston. Bissinger writes: "Brian looked at the east coast with a combination of curiosity and anthropological interest, as if he were studying a different species, and he concluded that it was no place for a human being to actually live."

I've often felt much like Brian as I try to understand education in the context of communities and cultures. Most places are unlike the small New Hampshire town where I lived, and I've struggled in trying to draw conclusions about whether a particular school is "good" or "bad." Mostly I feel they mirror the different values of people across the country. It's not my responsibility, nor within my competence, to judge them one way or the other.

It's OK with me if a school district wants to offer Bible classes and build an awesome stadium. If a school would rather build a greenhouse and teach ecology, or buy musical instruments and teach rhythm and blues, more power to it. Bissinger quotes the Odessa school superintendent, "'Public schools reflect a community's desires, feelings, dreams,' and nowhere did those dreams unfold more powerfully than they did on the football field." I can't argue with that.

March, 4, 2009
In the Shadow of the Mountain, Las Cruces, New Mexico

I left the Permian High School football stadium in Odessa and continued across southern Texas to the border town of Las Cruces, New Mexico, which is literally in the shadow of the Organ Mountains. Las Cruces was established by the U.S. Army when the territory was acquired following the Treaty of Guadalupe Hidalgo and the Gadsden Purchase. The view from my hotel room is stunning.

128

My drive took me past a billboard that advertised McDonald's chicken sandwich. I'm glad it showed a photo of the sandwich, because the ad contained no English. Maybe that's normal in the Southwest. Most of the radio stations seemed to broadcast in Spanish, and at the hotel I found I couldn't communicate with the woman cleaning rooms. A brochure in the lobby explained that Las Cruces is a fast-growing city whose population growth is driven by immigration. It's not just Las Cruces: In 2007 immigrants accounted for one in eight U.S. residents, the highest percentage in 80 years, and one in five of America's K-12 students is an immigrant or a child of immigrants.

I've been celebrating school diversity as a reflection of the culture of diverse communities. Nathan Glazer, author of *We Are All Multi-culturalists Now*, wrote that one advantage of schools of choice is that they "bring to the educational process the social capital that reflects the common values of a group of teachers, a community of parents, and their children—and...make education more effective by so doing." He warned that efforts to eliminate school differences would weaken "the advantageous consequences of the act of choice in creating the community in the first place."

Yet while diverse school cultures are welcome, school flexibility is not boundless, particularly when public money is involved. Taxpayers have expectations for their schools, and although they may differ community by community, finding a way to teach the nation's heritage ought to be one of education's goals. In his 1988 book, *Cultural Literacy*, University of Virginia scholar E.D. Hirsch explained that American children "enter neither a narrow tribal culture nor a transcendent world order but a national literate culture." Preparing children for that culture is an important function of education: "In the best of worlds, all Americans would be multiliterate. But surely the first step in that direction must be for all of us to become literate in our own national language and culture."

Indeed, to celebrate diversity we have to communicate with each other. Without a common language, Hirsch argues that the results will be "cultural fragmentation, civil antagonism, illiteracy and economic-technological ineffectualness." That's why bilingual education is a mistake. Hirsch writes that a "well-meaning linguistic pluralism, which would encourage rather than discourage competing languages within our borders, is much different from Jeffersonian pluralism, which has encouraged a diversity of traditions, values, and opinions. Toleration of diversity is at the root of our society, but encouragement of multilingualism is contrary to our traditions and extremely unrealistic."

Hirsch doesn't stop at support for English language education. He

129

favors education for "cultural literacy," which is, "the whole system of widely shared information and associations," that acts as the "oxygen of social intercourse." Unfortunately, Hirsch believes cultural literacy is declining: The "amount of shared knowledge that we have been able to take for granted in communicating with our fellow citizens" has fallen sharply.

The brief layover in Las Cruces started me thinking about the constraints placed on school choice by the broader public purposes of education. I look at Hirsch's Core Knowledge proposal in greater depth in the next chapter after visiting two schools in Colorado that use his curriculum.

March 6, 2009
Arizona Scholarship Fund, Mesa, Arizona

Chambria Henderson, the executive director of the Arizona Scholarship Fund, is a longtime supporter of tuition tax credits. The idea first came to her in high school during a history class discussion of the Boston Tea Party. Concerning taxation and representation, Henderson wondered, "What if you had full representation by being able to direct your tax dollars to wherever you want them to go?"

The Arizona Scholarship Fund (ASF) that she now heads is a school tuition organization that participates in the state's tuition tax credit program. It's the third largest, after programs run by the Arizona Christian School Tuition Organization and the Catholic diocese of Phoenix. Henderson, who has keen political instincts (and, she says, "skin like a rhino") helped craft the tax credit legislation in 1997. She believes the state program gives taxpayers more control over where their tax dollars are spent in education. With tax credits, citizens and companies contribute money to non-profits like Henderson's ASF, and reduce their taxes by the amount they give. The non-profit then provides scholarships to families to send their kids to a private school.

The tax credit is like a voucher program, with benefits provided to a donor intermediary. Under the Arizona program, credits are available to both individuals (capped at $500) and businesses ($10 million is the total amount available, set to expand to $20 million by 2011). In the ten years since the law's enactment, $293 million has gone to families for tuition assistance. (There is also a state program that provides a tax credit for gifts to public schools in support of extracurricular activities and character education. Public schools have received more than $263 million since 1997 through this program.)

The Arizona Supreme Court has ruled that the tax credit is constitutional, but the program is back in court over a challenge that its implementation violates the First Amendment. At issue are complaints that the program violates the separation of church and state. Henderson, who attended the court hearings, is surprisingly sympathetic to the argument by the plaintiff, the ACLU. She explained that she had wanted the tuition tax credit program to be very expansive. She imagined that the tax credit would help any parent pay for a private school education without regard to income, ethnicity, religion or any other restrictions. In practice, however, the program works differently. She said most of the 55 state-designated Scholarship Tuition Organizations, are little mom-and-pop shops devoted to a particular religious constituency. There is a Jewish scholarship fund and a Catholic scholarship fund. Browsing through the list of hundreds of schools receiving scholarships, I noticed that only a handful are not primarily religious.

Henderson was dismayed that the tax credit program had fostered religious sectarianism, but she accepts that it's the result of giving people freedom to choose. She predicts that other states will adopt programs like Arizona's.

Should education tax credits replace taxes for education?

In 2007 Arizona received and spent $9.6 billion in taxpayer dollars on elementary and secondary education. That's almost 200 times more than the $54 million in tuition tax credit assistance that went to Arizonans. The tax credit program is still small but it's growing steadily. Does it have the potential to do more, and could it serve as a foundation for a new way of funding education? Education analyst Adam Schaeffer of the libertarian Cato Institute supports education tax credits, which he calls, "the future for school choice, and it's looking pretty bright."

Cato's Schaeffer has written a study comparing vouchers to education tax credits—and he thinks tax credits are superior. Vouchers, he says, have several disadvantages. "In a voucher system, taxpayers have no direct control over how their money is spent. It all goes into one pot and is distributed according to the rules agreed to by the majority of legislators." Many people are likely to be quite upset if their taxes are used for programs or schools they oppose. Then politicians will put controls prohibiting voucher use for non-preferred purposes. "Over time, such regulations, added in response to periodic difficulties, accumulate until little freedom remains for education service providers," writes Schaeffer. Furthermore, "In a voucher system, the decision on whether or not to continue funding students at any particular school is made by the government acting through the political and legal processes, not by individuals interacting through market mechanisms within civil society."

Schaeffer argues that tax credits bypass these worries. I am not so sure. I think an extensive program of tax credits faces the same regulatory prospects and threats of political interference as vouchers. Schaeffer's ideal world in which only individuals decide where the money goes in education works only if there is no public funding of education. If Schaeffer sees tax credits as an intermediate step to do away with public funding for education, that's one argument. But as long as we have public funding, we will have politics. Already, Arizona scholarship funds that come from the corporate tax credit program are subject to strict guidelines that limit the recipients to those from low-income families.

It's no surprise that the tax credit program is popular in Arizona. School superintendent Calvin Baker, quoted in the *Tucson Citizen*, said, "'Private school parents and supporters love the benefit it gives private schools,' he said, 'and public school parents love it because it gives them a tax credit for the increasing large student sports and activity fees. Coaches and others love tax credits because they make fundraising so much easier,' Baker said. 'Spend Saturday supervising a car wash. . . or convince one parent to give the activity their tax credit - pretty easy choice.'"

Tax credits have a lot going for them. They help the family that "pays twice" for education, in taxes and again in private school tuition. They also give wealthy individuals and corporations greater say in how their education tax dollars are spent. If education tax credits expand, I bet private schools funded by the credits will come to resemble public charter schools, publicly funded but independently run. That sounds like a fine development.

Yet perhaps it's not all to the good. If state tax credits in Arizona give parents and taxpayers more control and choices—more freedom—why stop at Arizona? Wouldn't national education tax credits be the logical next step? I hope not. Such a move would consolidate power over education policy and centralize the administration of it. Then the only way for average citizens to change education policy would be to cast a vote in a federal election once every four years. Arizona citizens already have to go through Phoenix to voice their opinion about the state's tax credit program. I worry that transferring everyday schooling decisions into distant political ones will lessen society's vitality.

In his book *The Conservative Mind*, Russell Kirk, paraphrasing

Alexis de Tocqueville, wrote, "Whatever prevents the concentration of power is preservative of freedom and traditional life. In the United States, the federal framework, township government, and the autonomous judicial power all are means for ensuring this separation." Freedom cannot be sustained and exercised by individuals simply because government, even popularly elected, enshrines it. Power must be balanced by power, Kirk asserted, for individual and local freedom to flourish: "Astute lovers of freedom will assert state powers constantly, so that personal and local liberties may endure; the smaller the unit of government, the less possibility of usurpation, and the more immediate and powerful the operation of prescriptive influences."

Schaeffer and Henderson may be right that tax credit programs have the potential to proliferate across the states. Yet to the extent they weaken intermediary governments and institutions—towns, school districts, and counties—their effect may not be wholly positive. In most cases I don't think education tax credits will, or should, replace the existing system of locally-controlled and locally-funded public schools.

March 9, 2009
East Career and Technical Academy, Las Vegas, Nevada

Vo-tech in Vegas. East Career and Technical Academy (ECTA) is at the corner of Hollywood and Vegas Valley Drive in Las Vegas, Nevada. On a small hill east of the Strip, the school commands an impressive view of Sin City, with mountains rising behind it in the west. ECTA is in a magnificent new building (giant courtyard, modern-design staircase, suspended roof) that received an award for environmentally sustainable construction. This isn't your father's vo-tech high school.

Lisa Adler, the school's community partnership organizer, arranged for me to visit the school. We walked through a huge banquet hall and a beautiful commercial kitchen before visiting a top-of-the-line construction/electric/plumbing/welding workshop and auto body shop. ECTA's facilities would be the envy of any college.

There's a lot to admire about the idea of vo-tech education. Project-based learning and hands-on opportunities work better for many students than straight book learning. Former New York teacher of the year John Gatto writes, "After almost thirty years of classroom teaching I came to see what Benjamin Franklin must have realized as a teenager: Only a few of us are fashioned in such a peculiar way as to thrive on an exclusive diet of blackboard work and workbook work and bookwork work and talkwork work of all sorts."

Still, ECTA looked phenomenally expensive and underutilized, and it made me wonder what Gatto really meant when he argued that students ought to be "intermingling intimately with the real world of adults." How is having students "work with children" at school superior to being a nanny in the evening? How different is "learning the culinary arts" in school different from working at a local restaurant on weekends? Is auto shop class better than being an apprentice to a local mechanic?

The debate over the role of vocational education is an old one, but it has a new overlay. Americans recognize that brainpower is the ticket to prosperity in the modern economy. They say you "earn what you learn," and it's true. This economic reality goes a long way towards explaining the extravagant but prevailing belief that all students need a four-year college degree, which diminishes the old idea of vocational education. Knowing how to sew or hoe are not 21st century career paths for the masses, and everyone knows it.

But the college-for-all rhetoric is also contrary to reality. The fact is one-half of all students have to be below average. Encouraging everyone to go to college doesn't change the math, although it produces large numbers of students who fail to graduate. The pressure on young people to get more education obscures the reality that many students have no idea what kind of education they want or what they want to do with it. That's all the more reason why high quality vocational programs make sense, either at the high school or college level or through a training/apprenticeship model.

As Matthew Crawford points out in his insightful book, *Shop Class as Soulcraft*, competence in the "trades"—the work of the mechanic, plumber, and electrician—pays well, can't be outsourced, and it's intellectually engaging, more than most people think. I believe the winds are shifting on the value of vocational education.

The modern economy, Crawford contends, is based on cognitive stratification. Truly intellectual and creative tasks fall to a shrinking pool of elites, who codify their work into an efficient and uniform systems of rules and processes that govern what most people do for a living. It's a well-organized system and a productive one from which consumers benefit. But the jury is out on whether this system creates an economy in which a "diversity of human types can find work to which they are suited."

March 13, 2009
Honolulu, Hawaii

At first I thought I would visit one of Hawaii's private schools since the state has one of the highest private school attendance rates in the country. However, the two most interesting schools were not favorable to hosting my visit: the elite private Punahou School, which President Obama attended (it looked great from over the fence) and the Kamehameha Schools, the nation's wealthiest secondary school (its endowment rivals the most prominent universities).

So I switched my focus to Hawaii's public school system, which is just as interesting. Hawaii is unique among the 50 states in that its public education system isn't organized around local school districts. Hawaii has a single school district run by the State Department of Education. In size—257 public schools and 31 public charter schools enrolling 178,000 students—Hawaii's state school district is comparable to that of a mid-size city like Dallas. And unlike much of the rest of the country, education funding in Hawaii comes primarily from the state and federal governments, not from local property taxes. Public school assignment is still based on residence.

While there aren't school districts, Hawaii has adopted a policy that aims for flexibility and school-based decision making. It's a policy called Weighted Student Funding. In theory, the policy is simple. The state determines the "base" cost of educating a student (about $5,000 in Hawaii) and then calculates how much in increased funding students should receive based on individual factors such as residence, age, socioeconomic status, and English language ability. So, for instance, a rural school might receive $7,500 when parents of a 5th grade girl decide to send her there, while another school might receive $10,600 when it enrolls a poor boy learning English as a second language. Total spending per pupil averages out to about $9,000 per student. The "weighted" student funding follows the child to the public school where he or she is enrolled. School principals are granted considerable discretion over how they spend the funds. They don't have the right to accept or deny students.

The idea of Weighted Student Funding (WSF) has created odd political bedfellows because it splits the difference between two education concepts—vouchers and education "adequacy" lawsuits—that appeal to ideologically opposed constituencies. Supporters on the political left emphasize the potential of WSF to provide for more equity between schools by adding extra help for poor and minority kids. Supporters on the right argue that WSF will help schools decentralize and compete for students, providing more choices for parents. When the school choice-oriented Fordham Foundation issued a report, "Fund the Child," in 2006, announcing that the time for WSF "is now," signatories to it included Bush education secretary Rod Paige and John Podesta, Bill Clinton's chief of staff.

The libertarian Reason Foundation is on board with WSF. "Student-based funding is a system-wide reform that allows parents the right of exit to the best performing schools and gives every school an incentive to change practices to attract and retain families from their communities," writes Reason's Lisa Snell, who reported on the dozen cities using WSF around the country. Under WSF school principals have more decision-making authority, which trims central office costs. In other words, WSF acts like a public school voucher system, or a vast system of charter-like public schools, jostling and competing for students, constantly improving and quickly responding to parent demand.

The liberal Center for American Progress (CAP), which Podesta now heads, is also on board with WSF, enticed by Fordham's pronouncement that WSF is the "best hope for achieving equity." CAP's Cynthia Brown writes: "Now, why is weighted student funding needed? It's needed because the current system of public school funding is plagued by inequity and it is very old." Richard Kahlenberg of the liberal Century Foundation supports the idea on the ground that it will spur integration by helping poor kids go to middle class schools. He thinks WSF achieves the same end as education adequacy lawsuits and provides more resources for education, with most of the money following the students who are most disadvantaged.

As Abraham Lincoln said of the Civil War combatants, "We all declare for liberty, but in using the same word we do not all mean the same thing." The same could be said for WSF. Of course Weighted Student Funding can't be all things to all people. As the policy matures, who is going to like what they see? My hunch is that conservatives will be more frustrated.

Consider the question of who decides how much it costs to educate a student. In Hawaii, the task falls to The Committee on Weights, a group whose name could come from Orwell's novel *1984*. It is a group of educators, principals and community members selected by the state superintendent and state board of education. Similar "expert" panels are assembled to "cost out" funding whenever advocacy groups file education adequacy lawsuits, and it's difficult to imagine large-scale voucher programs without a group like it to decide voucher amounts.

Who loses?—mainly neighborhood school supporters who distrust complex systems created by "experts" and worry that the findings will frustrate local control and raise school costs. When WSF was implemented in Hawaii and some schools received less funding than under the prior arrangement, the State Legislature's response was to increase the education budget by $20 million to ease the pain for these schools.

In New York City there are already 50 different categories, or weights, in the funding formula, says Michael Rebell, a professor at the Teachers College at Columbia University. "It becomes a game. The politicians could reach out to whatever community they want to appeal to politically, say bilingual or gifted and talented, and say we're going to increase the amount for gifted and talented this year or for ELL so they give a little more in that pot," Rebell writes.

It's different with local school districts where district residents and local officials, usually an elected school board, argue through the issues. If the residents disagree, they can vote someone out of office. The system gives power to the common citizen.

Weighted Student Funding concentrates decision making in the Committee on Weights. The conversation over who gets what is dominated by the experts who are unelected. "Here," says University of New Hampshire professor Matthew Parks of unelected experts in general, "is our new class of masters."

March 30, 2009
West Ranch High School, Santa Clarita, California

Honolulu is a weird place to visit. Stuff is exorbitantly expensive, and the style of the place is so strange I almost felt I was in another country. On city streets Hawaiian locals mingle with beach bums and burn-outs, and tourists from cruise ships celebrate amid soldiers and sailors from nearby military bases. Although I had eagerly anticipated Hawaii, I was glad to be back on the mainland. As I enter the ninth month of the trip, I'm beginning to feel the toll of the road.

In Riverside, a suburb of Los Angeles, I came across a report just released by California's Pacific Research Institute (PRI). It was entitled, "Not As Good As You Think: Why The Middle Class Needs School Choice." The report laid out a familiar scenario: middle class parents move to a well-to-do suburban neighborhood, often paying through the nose for their home so their kids can attend a good public school. "Not as Good as You Think" looks at home prices and test scores at schools throughout California, and comes to a surprising conclusion: middle class families are being duped. Student test scores at "good" schools just aren't as good as they should be.

137

"In nearly 300 schools in middle class and affluent neighborhoods, more than half of the students in at least one grade level performed below proficiency on the 2006 California Standards Test (CST)," the report found. Not only does the report "shatter the myth" that these are good schools, it points out that things are actually "rotting inside these seemingly cozy cocoons." And parents are unaware of the bait-and-switch.

The report was interesting in that it focused on school choice but targeted wealthy suburbanites. Most advocates for school choice make a strong moral argument that the policy helps poor kids escape dismal city schools. But as I traveled across the country I was seeing resistance from suburban families who often liked their local public schools and were nervous about vouchers. The report's authors recognized that unless school voucher proponents convince California's broad middle class that their own public schools are failing school choice reform will have no chance of success.

In California, school voucher ballot initiatives failed in 1993 and 2000 by more than two-to-one margins. A study in the *Journal of Urban Economics* analyzed precinct results for Proposition 174, California's 1993 voucher initiative. It found that residents of good school districts in Los Angeles County disproportionately rejected vouchers. The authors concluded that L.A. voters were either trying to protect their home values or thought it was a referendum on the quality of their local public schools. After looking at the data, Dartmouth economist Bill Fischel wrote: "Vouchers were most soundly rejected in those places in California where local public schools have maintained their higher quality in the face of fiscal constraints."

I decided to visit a suburban public school to see how it measured up to the PRI report. West Ranch High School could well be one the schools PRI examined (though it's not). It scored well on California's Academic Performance Index (API), with a score of 818, compared to the California average of 710, and it certainly fit the description of a typical suburban upper-middle class school. It is in the William S. Hart school district, 35 minutes north of Los Angeles, in the "edge city" of Santa Clarita (population 180,000). Santa Clarita and nearby cities are predominantly white and wealthy. They consistently make the FBI list of the safest cities in the nation.

West Ranch, built in 2004 on 52 acres, sits in a valley amid green rolling hills. I was told that only four percent of the 2,600 students come from low-income families but could have guessed as much by eying the cars in the parking lot. Some 89% of West Ranch parents went to college. The average class size is a hefty 32 students, although there were only half as many kids in the senior elective class I visited, "Contemporary American Problems." The students seemed bright and earnest, respectful and, considering it was the first class of the day, surprisingly conversational. With their affluent backgrounds, it was perhaps predictable that they considered drug use, particularly pot, the most pressing problem facing America.

Perhaps suburban parents will be more receptive to vouchers and other choice-based reforms if they are persuaded that schools like West Ranch are far less successful then they imagine. At least that's PRI's hope. The group is targeting the right constituency, but its approach is problematic. For starters, it's tough to persuade parents that they are poor judges of their own kids' schools but will have the capacity to make informed, quality choices when they have access to vouchers.

The problem is that most parents think they know what kind of school they are getting for their tax dollars. For one thing, they know their child's classmates. And they believe their child's level of achievement is influenced by the kids their child goes to school with. They are right. The central finding of the influential 1966 "Coleman Report" has been reconfirmed in many studies: "The social composition of the student body is more highly related to achievement, independent of the student's own social background, than any other school factor."

What's paradoxical about vouchers is that while they give parents choice in picking a school for their child, they give other families the same choice, which includes the choice to send their kids to West Ranch. Parents picture busloads of children, many of them poor and Hispanic, on the freeway heading up to West Ranch, and say "hold on." Homeowners in the area, who recognize that housing prices are tied to perceived school quality, have similar reservations. Ironically, vouchers reduce the control West Ranch parents exercise over their child's classmates. Most parents at schools like West Ranch will say they are happy with their child's neighborhood-based school. That's often why they move to the neighborhood. And it's why they tend to veto voucher ballot initiatives. Telling parents that their kids aren't as smart as they should be is unlikely to alter that calculus.

* * *

April 3, 2009
Salt Lake City, Utah

I'd like to continue with the theme of why citizens vote down statewide voucher initiatives, so at this point I'm attaching the account of my visit to Utah in April.

In 2006, Utah's Republican Gov. John Huntsman signed into law a statewide education voucher bill that promised to help the parents of Utah's 512,000 public school students send their children to the school of their choice—public or private. The Parent Choice in Education Act was subsequently challenged and a referendum put the issue before the state's voters on November 6, 2007. A majority vote was needed to retain school choice.

Many observers thought Utah was sure to uphold school vouchers. Republicans tend to be more supportive of vouchers, and Utah is the most Republican state in the nation. Moreover, most voucher programs such as those in Milwaukee, Cleveland and Washington, D.C have been implemented in urban communities and, contrary to what you might suppose, Utah is the sixth most urbanized state in the nation, with almost 90% of the state's population living in the metropolitan area surrounding Salt Lake City. As I drove on I-80 across the desolate countryside of eastern Nevada and the barren salt flats of western Utah it was easy to understand why the countryside was so sparsely populated. It's the longest stretch of interstate without an exit (almost 40 miles) and large road signs warn drivers about fatigue and drowsiness.

On the other hand, school choice finds support among minorities. Although survey results of voucher support jump all over the map depending on how questions are phrased, overall the picture is one of greater support among minorities and the poor. In 2007 the journal *Education Next* found "Both African Americans and Hispanics are markedly more likely to support vouchers than are whites. Indeed, 68 percent of African Americans and 61 percent of Hispanics favor vouchers, compared to 38 percent of whites."

Stanford University's Terry Moe, referring to data on respondents' initial support for vouchers writes, "The modern thrust of the voucher movement is very much in evidence here. As we found in the aggregate, the parents who most favor vouchers are those who are low in social class, black or Hispanic, and from disadvantaged school districts." Utah is 84% white. Furthermore, Utah's public schools are popular—Utah has the fifth-highest proportion of K-12 students in public schools—and Utah schools rank near the top in achievement and other quality measures when compared to other states.

On voting day, Utah citizens overwhelmingly rejected the ballot initiative by a margin of nearly 2:1. Vouchers failed in all 29 counties, as well as in most districts represented by politicians who were ardent supporters of school choice.

What happened? On the eve of the referendum I wrote an article stating that if vouchers failed, it would be because of the money teacher unions and liberal interest groups poured into the campaign. I identified the National Education Association (NEA) as the principal opponent followed by a consortium called Utahans for Public Schools, which "added the political muscle of the Utah PTA, the ACLU and the local NAACP chapter to attack school choice." A George Will column also took the unions to task, accusing them of "waging an expensive and meretricious campaign to overturn the right of parents to choose among competing schools, public and private, for the best education for their children."

In retrospect, I'm no longer convinced that the battle was between parents and the unions. The NEA fought reform, but it didn't outspend the supporters of vouchers. In Utah, voucher proponent Patrick Byrne, founder of Overstock.com, contributed several million dollars to the campaign. As was the case in the 2000 California statewide voucher referendum, which failed by an even larger margin, voucher supporters spent as much as if not more than opponents.

The resounding rejection of statewide vouchers in Utah suggests that something else is at play besides the political clout of teachers unions. Why have large majorities voted down statewide voucher initiatives? Two related explanations deserve a hearing.

Social Capital

The first is made by Dartmouth economist Bill Fischel. In his 2004 article "Why Voters Veto Vouchers," Fischel argues that the benefits of neighborhood public schools accrue "largely to the parents of school children and to other adult residents of the community." When kids attend a local school, it allows "voting adults to get to know one another better, which in turn reduces the transaction costs of providing other local public goods." In other words, parents get to know other parents in their neighborhood.

It doesn't stop there. When adults know one another, they form groups around school and neighborhood issues. Parent groups "get in the way of school experiments like open classrooms and 'whole language' reading," and homeowner groups insist that "police pay attention to graffiti and excessive noise." These associations build what Fischel terms "community-specific social capital," the lubricant for local self-government.

Vouchers counter this effect. "By enabling parents to select schools outside their communities and outside of local public supervision," he writes, "vouchers work against the neighborhood and community networks that facilitate the bottom-up provision of local public goods." Fischel thinks many voters are disinclined to favor vouchers for this reason. "An inarticulate desire to maintain the network of intra-community links that public schools provide may account for voters' resistance to statewide voucher programs even in places where vouchers would seem to be most attractive."

I've witnessed something similar to what Fischel describes during my visits to public schools in small towns like White Lake, South Dakota; Lolo, Montana; and Houlton, Maine, and it seems likely that the argument also holds true in Utah. I looked at the county-by-county results of the voucher vote, and found that most rural Utah counties rejected vouchers by a significantly higher margin than the state average of 62%: Beaver County (Pop. 6,000) voted 80% NO; Carbon County (Pop. 20,000) voted 75% NO; and Emory County (Pop. 11,000) voted 78% NO.

Peer Effects

Fischel admits that his social capital theory can't fully explain voucher opposition in more urban areas. Residents of Salt Lake City County (Pop. 900,000) also opposed vouchers by a margin (67%) higher than the state average. In this case, I believe voucher opposition stems not only from parents' desire to know each other; it's also based on parents' desire to know their child's classmates and friends.

Parents believe the children who go to class with their sons and daughters will influence them and affect their levels of achievement. They are on to something. School and classroom dynamics are created by the students who walk through the schoolhouse door, a reality that I've observed in numerous school visits, and that the "Coleman Report" and other studies have demonstrated.

Because there are many school districts, because people are mobile and communities have zoning regulations, "local schools, though nominally in the public sector, became more like a private good," Fischel notes. "In order to get the benefits of the schools, you had to buy a home in the community whose property taxes covered the cost of education." In Utah local property taxes no longer have much impact on the quality of education; 71% of funding comes from the state and 11% from the federal government. But the aspect of schooling that parents most care about—influence over their child's classmates—remains a local matter.

In Utah and around the country, residential patterns reflect income. With neighborhood-based assignment, schools also reflect income. Schools in South Provo, Downtown Ogden, or on the west side of Salt Lake City, for example, are largely poor and minority. Schools in Alpine and Holladay are almost entirely wealthy and white. As Leah Barker, spokeswoman for Salt Lake City pro-voucher group Parents for Choice in Education, said, "How much more segregated can we possibly be? All the low-income families live in the west side (of the Salt Lake Valley) and attend failing schools. We are segregated right now based on income."

I couldn't find data on the breakdown of the voucher vote by Salt Lake City precinct, but my observations around the country lead me to believe parents' intuition about peer effects played a deciding role in the outcome of the Utah voucher vote. Vouchers give parents more choices, but they limit the control middle and upper class parents exercise—by choice of residence—over their child's classmates. Fischel points out that a voucher system has "many virtues in promoting more individual choice among families and creative competition among suppliers." Those benefits are real, but they come at a price, one that many citizens aren't prepared to pay, at least not statewide in Utah.

April 1, 2009
American Indian Public Charter School, Oakland, California

I left Santa Clarita, drove north across California's agricultural Central Valley to Oakland on the east side of San Francisco Bay. My destination was a unique place: The American Indian Public Charter School (AIPCS). Its founder, Ben Chavis, a Lumbee Indian from North Carolina, took over the disorderly and dysfunctional public school in 2000, fired most of the teachers and instituted a highly paternalistic culture. As columnist George Will wrote after a visit to the school, "Telling young people what they must do is what Chavis does."

The school's students are almost all from poor families in the Oakland area. Most are Asian, with a handful of blacks and Hispanics. The school is zealous about raising academic achievement as measured by California's Academic Performance Index, and scores at the school have more than doubled in just seven years (436 in 2000-2001 to 967 in 2007-2008). Now only four schools in the entire state of California score higher than AIPCS.

To earn these scores, the school has its own "Ten Commandments." Number one is "Thou shalt accept full responsibility for thy failure in school and life. Blaming thy family, friends or circumstances will not lead to success. Blame is an excuse for failure and laziness." While many charter schools I've visited practice a "No Excuses" approach, AIPCS takes it to the limit. "This is an Asian model," principal Janet Roberts told me as we sat in her office. And it's designed for poor minorities. "I don't use that middle-class rhetoric," Chavis once said. "I don't believe in building self-esteem, fundraising, parent involvement. My system is not for middle-class, upper-class whites."

Teachers also are held responsible. Roberts said that for the first few weeks of each school year she wants to hear kids say they hate their teachers because they are so demanding. Roberts only needs two interview questions to weed out teachers who won't fit her needs: "Was your family strict?" and "What is the highest level of math you've taken?" If teachers don't work out, Roberts is emphatic that the principal must have the power to fire them. "The kids love it when I fire a teacher." Teachers are paid more than their district counterparts and receive a bonus for boosting student achievement. It's not surprising that teacher turnover at the school is high.

Competition between students is encouraged, and failure is recognized publicly. "I love competition, I love embarrassment," said Roberts. As I toured the school's classrooms I saw several kids sitting on the floor amid other students sitting at desks. Roberts had the students explain to me the reasons why their desks were taken away: usually it was for not doing homework or poor attendance. Public humiliation is a powerful motivational strategy at AIPCS.

Roberts supports No Child Left Behind and "anything that gives us data," and she doesn't believe the "testing discriminates by race" argument—"only against unprepared people," she says. Indeed, Commandment #3 reads, "Thou shalt remember that standardized tests are not aware of anyone's skin color or sex." She is comfortable talking about race, something she may have learned from Chavis, whose brazen in-your-face attitude generated plenty of controversy before his retirement in 2007. "It's a reality wherever you go. You're going to be judged on race," Roberts says. When she sees Asians doing poorly she says, "Those are my people and they need to do better." Commandment #9 reads, "Thou shalt be aware that "affirmative action" for minorities is the most blatant form of racism in the United States."

While it's important to reject the group determinism implicit in affirmative action, it's also important to admit that children have widely varying gifts, interests and abilities. The fact is most of the students at AIPCS are the brightest of the bright, despite being from poor families. They enroll in gifted and talented summer programs and are on their way to top colleges. Acing the SAT takes more than hard work; it takes innate intellectual ability. In a knowledge driven economy, brilliant students from any race and class are genuinely lucky, and it's a mistake to encourage the smartest of them to think they are successful simply because they work harder than everyone else.

In his column George Will acknowledged the special character of the school: "Paternalism is the restriction of freedom for the good of the person restricted. AIPCS acts *in loco parentis* because Chavis, who is cool toward parental involvement, wants an enveloping school culture that combats the culture of poverty and the streets." In some ways I thought the school resembled a military boot camp: students spend most of the day and most of the year in a school that provides them with uniforms and instructs them in how to sit up straight, respect teachers, and present themselves appropriately. The school calls itself a family, and indeed it fulfills many family functions.

The expansive model of training children may work where families and community structures are depleted, but I'm glad more school haven't adopted—haven't needed to adopt—it. Roberts said Chavis once described himself as "the Indian Bobby Knight." Basketball fans know Knight for his intense coaching style and angry tirades, and for his great success in winning college basketball games. But famed North Carolina coach Roy Williams wins games too, and he is far more laid back. Even in an explicitly competitive environment, working with young adults who deliberately choose to play college basketball, the two coaches employ very different styles. Now consider how different this is from K-12 public education, where attendance is compulsory, students' abilities and dispositions run the gamut, rules vary and the goals for success are unclear or disputed by parents and teachers.

I've noticed during my school visits that a big difference between private and public schools is that private schools embrace a single unifying principle or purpose. Parents choose a private school because they believe in the school's stated mission, and private schools enroll students who aren't going to detract from it. Charter schools and other public "schools of choice" try to imitate private schools in this way. Oakland, California parents who want a public school that provides all-encompassing discipline, competition, and rigor in their child's education have that choice in AIPCS.

CHAPTER SIX

Homeward Bound:
Pride and Provincialism
April 2 – May 13

Contoocook Valley New Hampshire Regional High School

It's April and I'm driving west to east on the last leg of my trip, going from central California across the heartland and then back home to New Hampshire. On this final segment I began by visiting a public school in Reno, Nevada, that only accepts the most academically gifted students. Is a "genius high" for the "gifted" discriminatory and elitist? Then in Colorado I looked into two public elementary schools that emphasize civics and the liberal arts, a core curriculum that used to be the standard model for education. What does it mean for public education when "core knowledge" is considered a specialized curriculum that parents choose for their children?

In Wichita, Kansas, I stayed with two homeschooling families who believe in the public benefits of education but not in the institution of government schools. My school year ended with my return to the public high school I attended in New Hampshire. My school. I found in myself the same provincial pride I saw expressed across America in so many students, parents and teachers toward *their* schools. Education reformers often worry that "school spirit" seems to blind Americans to education's many problems. To the contrary, I've concluded that schools cannot succeed without it.

146

April 2, 2009
Davidson Academy, Reno, Nevada

"I have always been committed to working with underrepresented, overlooked populations," said Colleen Harsin, the director of Davidson Academy. No, she wasn't talking about an inner city school serving the minority poor. "At the Davidson Academy," she continued, "I am able to make a positive difference for parents, children and our community by helping profoundly intelligent young people find their place in the world."

Davidson Academy is the Harvard of high schools located smack dab in the middle of the University of Nevada campus at Reno. It occupies the old memorial union building. My tour guides laughed as they pointed to where the couches and pool tables used to be. Not anymore. Davidson advises that eligible middle or high school students must "score in the 99.9th percentile on an IQ test, or score at the extreme for their age or grade on an aptitude test (SAT I, ACT or Explore)."

With its focus on rigor and selectivity, Davidson is tacking against the prevailing educational winds. Harsin is angered when people call it an elitist institution. "Giving support where support is needed is not elitist," she counters. "We don't put them on a pedestal," she said. Harsin cautioned that while Davidson students are academically gifted, they're still kids. Like all children they need structure and support as they move through adolescence.

Davidson Academy has the funding it needs to provide an education that is individually tailored to gifted kids in middle and high school. As a public school, it receives the same per-pupil funding allotment from the state—about $6,500—as other public schools in Nevada. But that isn't nearly enough to cover the nearly $22,000 that the school spends per pupil. The nonprofit Davidson Institute and other supporters of gifted education make up the difference, providing a tuition-free education for all students who qualify. Davidson has 70 students this year and plans to enroll 200 in the near future.

Each student has a personalized learning plan similar to the Individualized Education Plans (IEP) common in special education. Davidson has no grade levels as students are grouped by ability in each subject. I spoke with an English teacher who said ability grouping makes a huge difference: It is "much easier to have different ages than different abilities." A math teacher agreed, saying the biggest difference between Davidson and Reno High School, where he previously taught, was that "here you can throw something out there and it will stick with most kids. At Reno you have to pitch everything at three different levels."

Students learn with their intellectual peers at Davidson because of the school's selective admissions procedures and its practice of grouping by ability. That makes teaching and learning easier, and it has other benefits too. "It's possible that only being surrounded by smart people could make you elitist," the English teacher told me, "but I've seen more of a humbling effect." In their old schools many of the kids were the oddities, big fish in a small pond. Many parents feel a sense of relief that their children have found their niche at last. At Davidson there is tolerance for the smart kid who is only one of many.

Classmates matter. When I was in high school, my favorite class was Advanced Placement U.S. History. My public high school offered three levels of history, and students had to test into AP. Although I gave it no thought at the time, the class discussions, assignments and expectations worked for me because they worked for my classmates as well. It's what sociologists call "peer effect," and what I saw of it at Davidson reinforced my conviction that it is a key element in schooling.

Peer effect manifests itself in many ways. Economists Scott Carrell of UC-Davis and Mark Hoekstra of the University of Pittsburgh recently completed a study of the spillover effects of disruptive students on their classmates. "Our results confirm," the authors write, "first, that children from troubled families...perform considerably worse on standardized reading and mathematics tests and are much more likely to commit disciplinary infractions and be suspended than other students. We find also that an increase in the number of children from troubled families reduces peer student math and reading test scores and increases peer disciplinary infractions and suspensions." The researchers confirm what we already know from experience and common sense. As one commenter on Joanne Jacob's blog has observed, "A dancing nudist at Easter Mass, a screaming ape in a choir, or a disruptive student in a classroom all have a negative impact on the mission at hand...worship, sing or learn."

The peer effect is sometimes overlooked in academic debates over school choice. Parents, however, know their children's classmates are an important determinant of school quality and student achievement, and they want a measure of control over that factor. As I've seen elsewhere on this trip, a parent's silent question is: What's the use of being able to select your child's school if you have no input on your child's classmates? The important thing isn't the school building, or even who runs the school but rather, who goes to school with my kid?

I'm not making the argument that children should go to school only with others just like them. Real diversity—exposure to different ideas and people of different backgrounds—is an important part of education.

148

But the fact is parents do consider their child's classmates when they choose a school. It's an important factor in their decision, one that's received little attention in debates over improving education.

Excellence and Equality

Davidson's Harsin worries that the current national trend is going against gifted programs. "I'm confident about that," she said. The Belin-Blank Center for Gifted Education at the University of Iowa, agrees. Its 2004 report, "A Nation Deceived," argued that America's public schools are holding back the nation's gifted. Why? One reason is that "political and cultural pressures homogenize the learning needs of individuals and we pretend that there are no meaningful learning differences."

The No Child Left Behind law is a product of the political and cultural pressures for homogenizing school populations. Because NCLB mandates that all students reach the same level—proficiency— teachers are pressured to focus attention on "bubble" children, those who test near proficiency, at the expense of high and low achieving students. With the approach of NCLB's 2014 deadline for achieving what the law calls "universal proficiency," there will be increased pressure on schools to make sure that everyone passes. Unfortunately, the law, which aims to make student test scores rise, is likely to cause testing standards to fall. All-out efforts to achieve 100 percent "proficiency" can't help but produce mediocrity and won't help America's brightest students.

There is another, less obvious reason why the law hurts bright students. NCLB requires that schools break down test score results by particular group demographics: sex, race and socio-economic status. When scores are "deaggregated," schools will be penalized unless all groups test comparably. The NCLB requirement encourages teachers and schools to evaluate whether kids are learning in relation to their group identity—blacks and whites, rich and poor, boys and girls. When teachers and schools feel pressured to help students because of their group identity rather than fulfill their individual needs and potential, smart students—no matter their race, sex, or income level—will lose out.

Across the Desert

I thought about these issues as I drove across the long barren stretch of eastern Nevada into Utah. My brother had left me to finish his senior year of college, so I lost my traveling companion and was on my own. The sun set behind me as I headed east, turning the desert an incandescent gold. A nearly full moon rose, shedding soft silver light on the sand. It was a long and lonely drive but the pure emptiness and the brightness of the moon lent energy to a traveler. I zoomed along with the windows down and the desert air rushing by.

What sets people on edge about gifted education? During my travels I've become increasingly aware of the perception gap between social classes. Many people have a gnawing sense that the modern economy blesses an intellectual elite and ignores or penalizes those who are not part of it. The "knowledge economy" they call it, and it rewards the smart. Despite all the talk about the power of education to prepare students for the new economy, Americans are concerned that its fruits are only for the elite.

In his introduction to Alexis de Tocqueville's *Democracy in America*, Professor Harvey Mansfield underscores what that French visitor noted more than a century and a half ago:

"The most efficient production of consumer goods requires both concentration of capital—large corporations—and specialization of labor—small, repetitive tasks. This kind of production gives rise to inequalities not just in the incomes but eventually in the very abilities of workers and managers. Repetition of small tasks narrows one's mental faculties, whereas the challenge of managing a large corporation may enhance them. Tocqueville forsees the possibility of an industrial aristocracy based almost exclusively on intellectual ability, the new sort of aristocracy we now call meritocracy... Democracies will either have to swallow the new kind of inequality for the sake of maximizing material prosperity, or else accept diminished economic productivity for the sake of equality. No wonder the Americans Tocqueville portrays are anxious and frustrated!"

Americans have an ingrained belief that education will lift everyone above the average, so the perception of escalating disparities is at the root of the protest against gifted education. Of course, the mission of education is to challenge all students to realize their fullest capacity. But it's ludicrous to expect education to equalize student academic abilities. We only tell ourselves education can do this because we don't want to confront the unpleasant trade-off that Mansfield and Tocqueville recognized.

My cell phone started to vibrate, startling me with its rumble in the silent hours. In time I arrived in Salt Lake City and pulled into the parking lot of a sprawling and dirty Motel 6 near the airport. It was past two in the morning. A pale and bleary-eyed woman drinking Mountain Dew was at the check-in counter. The room I was given was damp and the sheets were dingy. I slept fitfully and periodically went to the window to check whether my car had been busted in again, as in Chicago. When I awoke at dawn wet snow was falling. I made a cup of instant coffee, and set off for Colorado.

April 6, 2009
Dennison Elementary School, Denver, Colorado

Most of the schools I've visited of late have been high schools, where the disagreements about educational means and ends have produced more school options. Students and parents now have more freedom of choice than they used to in selecting school structures and curricula. This is a fine development in secondary schooling, but what about primary schools? In Colorado, I sought out two elementary schools committed to the principle that a core body of American culture—stories and myths, history and literature—should be taught to all students. Interestingly, neither school was a traditional public school. Both were public "schools of choice."

The Jefferson County school district covers the suburbs west of Denver. For the most part, the school district follows a standard neighborhood assignment policy: Students whose parents live in neighborhood "A" attend neighborhood school "A." But the county also operates schools like Dennison Elementary. These so-called "option schools" accept students across neighborhood lines. They are comparable to what other districts call magnet schools.

Pam Benigno, who works for the Independence Institute, Colorado's market-oriented state public policy think-tank, introduced me to Dennison Elementary, a public option school founded in 1974. Its founding document reads, "The purpose of education is to convey an essential body of cultural knowledge to the next generation, and...a solid liberal arts education is required in order for all citizens to be effective participants in their communities."

Dennison principal Kathy Krieger told me achieving those purposes requires consistency and uniformity, which she considers the key reason why her school is effective. Trying to do everything is the "kiss of death." That's a message I've heard from school leaders around the country, from charter school founders to Catholic school principals. Educators tell me that juggling multiple goals, meeting the needs of diverse students in a single class or a single school, is among the most difficult tasks they face.

Krieger told me most Dennison parents have firm ideas about

151

education, and they have high expectations for what it should achieve. Parents expect Dennison to move their kids from "proficiency" to an "advanced" level. Like Davidson Academy in Reno, Dennison illustrates an important argument for a certain kind of school choice: Student success requires that schools be free to nurture a common purpose.

For Dennison the purpose of education is to convey an "essential body of knowledge" through a "solid liberal arts education." But this puts Dennison at odds with other kinds of education. Does a purely vocational education—say, a school that trains students to be computer programmers—make the cut? Does it fulfill the "purpose of education"? The Dennison model of rigorous study of core academic subjects used to be the standard model for education. (Think of "grammar school," a once common but now nearly obsolete term.) Now it's only one choice among many available to students.

April 7, 2009
Traut Core Knowledge, Ft. Collins, Colorado

After Dennison I visited an option school in Ft. Collins, Colorado, called Traut Core Knowledge. With 525 students in grades K-6, it is one of several schools in the city that offers a "Core Knowledge" curriculum. Like the Dennison curriculum, the purpose of the Core Knowledge series is to convey an essential body of American cultural knowledge. Developed by University of Virginia emeritus professor E.D. Hirsch, the curriculum was originally designed to help disadvantaged minority children acquire knowledge fundamental to a national literate culture that they might otherwise not get at home. It is ironic that Core Knowledge schools like Traut serve a very different school population— middle class white kids whose parents worry that they won't learn about ideas and traditions that were once held in common.

Traut, which opened in 1993, has been caught up in jurisdictional disputes. Some parents seeking more school independence unsuccessfully proposed to convert it from an option school to a charter school. The dissidents broke away to form the Liberty Common Charter School, also with a Core Knowledge focus. Meanwhile other families moved to be nearer to Traut, attracted to its reputation for excellence, and they unsuccessfully petitioned the board of education to make Traut a neighborhood school. Currently 54% of Traut students live within a two-mile radius of the school, and almost 90% live within a five-mile radius.

Principal Mark Wertheimer is a burly man sporting a black cowboy hat. He told me he was happy with the school's status as an option school. It provides what he considered a happy medium of flexibility, oversight and support. Wertheimer also stressed Traut's commitment to character development. Speaking of his own children, he said, "I want my kids to be smart and good, but good is more important." By all conventional measures, Traut is a fine school; it was recently named a National School of Character. Traut students do well on state tests, and there is a long enrollment waiting list numbering in the hundreds.

A quality staff, a core curriculum and character education—all figure prominently at Traut. But Wertheimer says it's the school's students and their families that make it successful. When he walks into a classroom Wertheimer says he can tell whether kids are from solid or troubled homes. "The most serious problem facing education," he continued, "is the breakdown of the family." Testing, accountability structures and all the rest are merely "secondary issues." While Traut has gone through bruising battles over its legal status, it's noteworthy that Traut's principal believes his students' home life is the most important factor in its success.

Can the notion that there are certain things all kids should learn be reconciled with local control and parental choice? I think so. Wertheimer insists that his school is successful because his students come from solid families. For this reason, his students are likely to learn at home the core body of cultural and civic knowledge that the school prides itself on conveying. But students who don't acquire this knowledge at home are less likely to attend schools that teach it. These obstacles are tough to overcome, but they are not insurmountable. Most parents believe their kids' success requires that they find a place for themselves in American life. Cultural literacy doesn't guarantee this, but it is a sine qua non.

April, 10, 2009
Homeschooling Families, Wichita, Kansas

In Colorado I heard debates over what should be taught in public schools, but no one made an argument against public schools. I encountered that argument when I read *Dumbing Us Down: The Hidden Curriculum of Compulsory Schooling*, a book by John Taylor Gatto, who in 1991 was named New York's Teacher of the Year.

In accepting his award, Gatto shocked his audience by announcing that he was retiring from teaching so he would no longer "hurt kids to make a living." Gatto described the defects of a public education system in which he felt complicit: "Government schooling is the most radical adventure in history. It kills the family by monopolizing the best times of childhood and by teaching disrespect for home and parents."

He argued that the institution of the public school fragments society, separating the young from the old, and contributes to family and community breakdown. "School is a major actor in this tragedy," he wrote. Compulsory, bureaucratic schooling leads to the "lessening of individual, family, and community importance."

These radical ideas resonate with families that homeschool their children—parents like Bob and Loretta Quinn, who made the decision to homeschool their five children. The Quinns and their children live with horses, a goat, and a garden a few miles north of Wichita, Kansas. When I sat down with Loretta on a clear spring day in April, she explained Gatto's message of fragmentation and separation. Children used to be educated mostly at home, she said, until the switch to what she termed the "industrial model" of education, which aimed to train kids to be dependable—and dependent—workers. By separating children from family and community, the new model removed them from the experiences necessary for a complete education, which is why Quinn says she chose to homeschool them.

Not opposed to all schooling models, Loretta Quinn recently started a private school using a classical education curriculum. The school has about eighty children but doesn't accept first and second graders in order not to encroach on family life. Quinn was fortunate to find an old factory building for the school, which she has refurbished into classrooms, a library and basketball gym. "Our little school of 80 kids is holding corporatism at bay," she laughs.

Tony and Celeste Woodlief live down the road from the Quinns, and they too homeschool their four sons. Tony Woodlief explains the family's decision: "Folks in our neck of the woods embrace the proper goal, which is supporting public education—not public schools—the education of the public, which means you and me and our neighbors. The goal is to educate children after all, not allegiance to some institution or ideology."

The kids played basketball outside as I sat with the Woodliefs around their kitchen table. Celeste, who once taught in Detroit public schools, is Montessori-trained and believes the approach has much to offer. Maria Montessori believed children have an innate interest in learning that is sparked by interactions with the environment. Contrary to some critics, that doesn't mean Montessori ignores structure, rules and discipline. The foundation of good parenting and education, writes Woodlief, "is love, order, and relentless application of rules: Eat all your vegetables, and Mind your manners, and Don't push your brother's head into the toilet." Tony attributes much bad parenting and inept schooling to the mistaken idea that children are inherently angelic. "Rather than help our children develop internal constraints that channel their energy and

154

passion into productive enterprises, we end up teaching them that limits and discipline are for chumps."

Tony and Celeste manage their time and hold their children's attention. While answering my questions, they get the kids dressed for church ("Are you sure you changed your underwear?"), and put dinner on the table ("Don't spill the soup on your nice shirt!"). Homeschooling takes lots of effort, and it's not always fun. But homeschooling families like the Quinns and the Woodliefs are proud to be responsible for their children's education. It's the stuff of life.

Charles Murray, the scholar whose influential writings have helped reform government welfare policy, argues that government takes away "too much of the life from life." Delivering the 2009 Irving Kristol lecture at American Enterprise Institute, Murray said:

The problem is this: Every time the government takes some of the trouble out of performing the functions of family, community, vocation, and faith, it also strips those institutions of some of their vitality—it drains some of the life from them. It's inevitable. Families are not vital because the day-to-day tasks of raising children and being a good spouse are so much fun, but because the family has responsibility for doing important things that won't get done unless the family does them. Communities are not vital because it's so much fun to respond to our neighbors' needs, but because the community has the responsibility for doing important things that won't get done unless the community does them. Once that imperative has been met—family and community really do have the action—then an elaborate web of social norms, expectations, rewards, and punishments evolves over time that supports families and communities in performing their functions. When the government says it will take some of the trouble out of doing the things that families and communities evolved to do, it inevitably takes some of the action away from families and communities, and the web frays, and eventually disintegrates.

Homeschooling is not for every family, but Murray's argument seems central to the outlook of many parents who homeschool their children.

March 23 – 24, 2009
ConVal Regional High School, Peterborough, New Hampshire

Home at last. Consciously or not, I sensed that ConVal Regional High School was the model against which I measured other schools. What would I think of my old school after the passage of time and the experience of visiting so many schools around the country?

155

I had made the trip to ConVal many times—as a student, on the school bus and in my first car, a '93 Subaru station wagon, and as a substitute teacher—down and across the bridge from Antrim, my hometown, past Bennington and Hancock.

Twenty miles from home to school is an unusually long trip, but ConVal (Contoocook Valley) is a regional high school, which means it serves nine small towns in southwest New Hampshire. With a thousand students, ConVal is a mid-sized, or Class I, public high school. The building that loomed large and sprawling in my high school memory now appears underwhelming. Late winter is an ugly time in New Hampshire. The trees are bare and mounds of dirty snow mixed with sand and salt line the roadways and loom in the corners of parking lots. Frost heaves—cracks in the highway road—take their toll on your vehicle, and everything appears worn down by the cold.

After visiting scores of teachers and principals at schools across the country, would I be disappointed by my own school? I didn't want that. My own experiences in high school were both rewarding and trying. I had great teachers and lousy ones, but overall I recall my time there fondly. The school served me well and I was proud of it because it was my school.

Why do we feel pride? In his introduction to Tocqueville's *Democracy in America* Harvey Mansfield wrote: "It is not just a few great general needs that are universal to human beings; so too is willful pride." Mansfield meant that people's lives aren't shaped only by wants and needs, over which they have little control, but by "certain distinct forms peculiar to a people of which they are proud." It struck me that schools are among those distinct forms that evoke powerful feelings of pride. They give people a sense of belonging to place, and place is always particular.

Tocqueville marveled at the "decentralizing passion" of Americans, their attachment to their communities and states. Daniel Webster embodied it in 1818 in his ringing defense of the independence of Dartmouth College: "It is, Sir, as I have said, a small college. And yet there are those who love it!" Many education reformers chide Americans for their stubborn attachments to local public schools and wonder how schooling can be improved when people look through rose-colored glasses at the schools of their youth. If only they would stop clinging to schools as they imagine they used to be, thinking that's what they now are.

I suspect most Americans don't resist changes to the structure of schooling merely for the sake of nostalgia. They reject the dictation of courts and "experts." Local residents respond, "No thank you. We'll take care of ourselves."

School districts may not be an efficient way to administer public education, but they do something more important. Mansfield again: "Tocqueville commends America's many local governments and nongovernmental associations not for their efficiency or even their justice, but because they develop citizens' attachment to political freedom." Locally controlled school districts squarely fit that description. They are among the "secondary powers" Tocqueville commends for filling the void between the individual and the state: they train citizens in the art of being free.

My visit to ConVal proved surpassingly informative and enjoyable in large part because of Principal Sue Dell. Dell began by talking about how ConVal is changing. More individualized instruction is becoming the norm, and with NCLB requiring that all kids reach the level of "proficiency," the responsibility of schools and teachers is shifting. "The days of planning a lesson for a whole classroom are quickly disappearing."

From day-to-day Dell says she must jump from one task to the next. "You have to be sort of ADD to be a principal," she laughs. "It's a real people business," that begins by greeting students as they arrive in the morning. Dell visits classrooms, handles teacher grievances, raises private money for lights for the football field, and holds weekly meetings with the district superintendent. She emphasized the importance of building and maintaining relationships based on trust.

Talking with Teachers

Dell arranged for me to speak with several ConVal teachers who agreed that the school was changing its ways. Teachers, prodded by parents, expected all kids to do well and believed most would go to college. Some parents push for scaled grades so their kids' scores look better for college admission, veteran math teacher Mary Clark told me, even though, she added, "not all kids have a reason to go." But across America less than 60% of incoming college freshman graduate after six years. That, said English teacher Bruce Thompson, could be a sign that we are pushing too many kids toward higher education.

Social studies teacher Donna Jacobs said education is prone to fads. She gets frustrated when schools are forced to jump "from bandwagon to bandwagon." However, Jacobs doesn't fault those pushing new initiatives to make things better: "It's generated out of the feeling, 'We have to do a better job'." Still, she believes silver bullet reforms take up teachers' time and usually fail. Jacobs says there just isn't enough time to do all she'd like for her kids.

On matters of school structure, Jacobs questioned the benefits of teacher tenure. You need to be a good teacher no matter how long you've been teaching, she said. Jacobs was open to the idea of merit pay, but wondered how it would work in practice. "Teaching is a very easy job to do badly, and very difficult to do well," but measuring and rewarding teachers for performance is no easier. She certainly supports more teacher observation and evaluation: "I've been observed once in 11 years." More evaluation would be an incentive to "ramp things up" in the classroom.

"When I think about how education has changed," journalist turned English teacher Bruce Thompson began, "I think more about how society has changed." Thompson is a middle-aged man with short-cropped grey hair whose clear manner of speech is the result of a career working with words. His observations about society were anchored in his experiences at ConVal and in southwest New Hampshire.

Society has gotten "cruder," Thompson noted, and ConVal kids show it. Crudeness is translated into lack of respect, an issue that came up frequently in my conversations. Teachers used to expect and receive respect from almost all students, but "those days are long gone." Now teachers tend to feel they must earn students' respect, and show students an equal measure of respect. A hierarchical relationship of teacher and student has become more egalitarian.

Math teacher Mary Clark attributed the increasing disrespect to broken homes, a decline in church attendance and other cultural markers. Thompson said the economic downturn hadn't helped. When parents are unemployed all sorts of bad things happen. While expressing reservations about current trends, Thompson was careful not to paint an overly rosy picture of the "good old days." Moreover, kids need to rebel. When Thompson gets into arguments with bad-mouthing kids he reminds himself, "It's not about me." Problems at home are usually the issue, he said.

As for the kids with a bad attitude—"Who cares where Zimbabwe is, I didn't have breakfast"—Jacobs notes that teachers knew more about their students' family problems twenty years ago. "Maybe we knew too much," Jacobs shrugged, "but now we know too little. "You can't educate the kids without knowing the whole person."

Clark told me her struggles with disrespectful students occur most frequently in classes for low-performing students. That reminds me of something Thompson told me: The distribution of students by academic achievement is changing. He called it the "U-Curve" phenomenon. Instead of a bell curve distribution, where most students are in the mid-range of academic achievement, Thompson notices lots more As and Bs, and lots of Ds and Fs, but "the C's have gone away." Thompson thinks society is losing its middle ground. The A and B students come from intact families that own books and have high expectations. That's not the case for D and F students.

Still, Thompson said he's "one of the few who think[s] public education is pretty good." Kids grow up, have families, find jobs and pay taxes. He cited research that Americans give their local schools a decent mark but worry about education overall. Forty-three percent give their local public school a grade of A or B (and 38% award a C). Only 20% award an A or B to American education in general.

Jacobs thinks school is the only place to meet people of different backgrounds and experiences. "You don't have the bank anymore, the church, or the town meeting." Perhaps ConVal serves that purpose, but my visits to public schools across America tell me the romantic notion of public schools as "common schools" is largely mythical, or at least historical. Taken collectively, public schools may reflect society overall, but looked at individually our schools reflect only their own neighbor-hoods, which means they reflect our society's social divisions by wealth and by race. Why this is so is subject to great debate. For Charles Murray residential and school patterns reflect a form of social sorting by intellectual ability, and Harvard sociologist Robert Putnam argues that self-segregation is a defense mechanism protecting "social capital," the common knowledge that builds trust and reduces conflict in communities.

I believe the role of school must be put into perspective. "Many adults in the community," Thompson said, "lose sight of the fact that most of what we know as adults, we didn't learn in high school." He notes that when ConVal asked parents what high school should teach their children the result was a great list of things from reading and math to character education, shop class and driver's ed. The list represented the parents' attempt to provide their children with the wisdom they would need to avoid "failure" and achieve "success." The fact is, however, that you rarely learn that in high school. You learn it in life.

Education's Promise

"I bet it was bad. Does our education system suck as much as everyone says? I think it's really sad." A Dartmouth student voiced this commonplace opinion after I described my project upon returning to New Hampshire. When I would question friends and neighbors to learn their opinion of American education, I often heard them admit to the woeful inadequacy of our schools.

159

Are our schools terrible, and, if so, what can be done to fix them? My initial response is: No, most schools aren't terrible, although it's easy to see why people think they are. Popular disappointment with schools is a product of the fantastic notions many people hold about their capacity to make children smarter and more successful. Especially among the well-educated who are accustomed to rapid technological and scientific change there is an expectation that education makes possible a rapid increase in productivity and efficiency—from the man with the hoe to the woman in an air-conditioned tractor listening to an iPod. But true education frustrates because the school's "end product," if we must use the term, is a human being. People can't be improved as easily as farm equipment.

To the extent that we are malleable, the social dynamic of the family and the community are most powerful. Schools mirror society more than they mold it. Inflated rhetoric to the contrary, what happens outside school is more influential than what happens inside it.

Does this mean we should give up on school reform? Certainly we should give up the widespread and pernicious notion that schools should raise all students to a common level of high academic competence. Because a modern economy rewards the smart and educated it's not popular to point out that half of all children must inevitably be "below average." But it's foolish for schools to think in these terms. Forcing all students to work toward a single standard of "achievement" will bore the brightest students, discourage the slowest ones, and give schools incentives to become intellectually dishonest.

That doesn't mean we shouldn't insist that schools instruct American children in a basic core program of studies, at least until 8th grade. That means English and Math, but also the historical texts, knowledge and lore that constitute our shared national culture. Broad literacy in this shared culture gives students the vocabulary that will enable them to communicate with one another across the economic, racial and geographic clans into which we cluster. It binds us together as one people. *E Pluribus Unum*.

School reform should be put in a broader context. Schools don't stand alone but are at the intersection of two institutions that matter more in rearing and educating children—the family and community. A sensible approach to school reform must first address how changes to school structure and education policy affect them.

As I have learned, it's not easy to decide how to give parents and community members the freedom and the authority to make education decisions. What parents want can be in conflict with the interests of others in the community and with other parents. No school reform will satisfy everyone or work everywhere.

Still, parents must push their legislators to sponsor more school choice options—from charter schools to a greater variety of school voucher programs that allow children to attend religious and non-religious schools. Private scholarship programs and tax credit scholarships are helping many students, but more government-funded vouchers can extend choice to children, especially the poor and minorities, trapped in failing public school systems. The defeat of statewide voucher ballot initiatives cannot become an excuse to give up on efforts to promote school choice. It is particularly tragic that Congress has been unwilling to extend an existing school voucher program that has enabled several thousand poor and minority children to choose alternatives to Washington, DC public schools.

But if we can accept the inadequacy of any comprehensive program for school reform, then we have taken the first steps to understanding what is more important for educating children. Pundits decry the unwieldy nature of local control, school inequalities and dispersed power over policy. But diversity in schooling is precisely what makes choice possible. Where there are local public schools, private schools, home-schooling, charter schools and other options available to parents and community members there is likely to be a greater "we'll take care of our own" spirit of self-reliance and communal responsibility.

When de Tocqueville traveled across the United States 170 years ago, he wrote about America's distinctive penchant for forming groups and associations. These institutions and allegiances are the components of civil society. They include both private and local public schools. They order society and fulfill communal needs while maintaining the freedom of choice that allows diverse groups to flourish.

Modern government and social science have introduced standardization and centralization into education. Testing is more efficient and precise because of administrative rulemaking and quantitative measures. But the robust civil society that Tocqueville identified as America's saving grace is weakened when school bureaucrats overturn the judgments and choices of families and communities. And schools won't achieve the multiple and various goals that parents and neighbors expect of them.

The stories I heard around the country are not all discouraging. I believe many Americans want to reserve a generous sphere of responsibility for themselves and their neighbors. They continue to cherish the value of "the little platoon we belong to in society," and yearn for it to be strong and important. Good education policy will give wings to these longings.

NOTES

In keeping with the style of this book, I omit endnotes in the text and use these notes to guide readers to my sources. Much of the statistical information comes from the website of the National Center for Education Statistics (NCES). Statistics concerning particular schools, school districts and states frequently come from their respective websites. URLs were accessed between September 2008 and December 2009.

I've often turned for guidance to the journal *Education Next*, an excellent reference on a wide-range of education topics. It can be accessed online at URL: (http://educationnext.org/journal/). Several books also figured prominently in influencing my ideas. Charles Murray's *Real Education* (Crown, 2008) is essential for an honest discussion of academic ability and its implications for education. Erick Hanushek's and Alfred Lindseth's *Schoolhouses, Courthouses and Statehouses* (Princeton University Press, 2009) brings together everything you need to know about school financing and the courts' involvement in it. For a discussion of why voters so often reject school voucher ballot initiatives I suggest two articles: "Why Voters Veto Vouchers" by William Fischel and "The Political Economy of School Choice" by James Ryan and Michael Heise. Both articles are available in full online. Unquestionably the book that had the greatest impact on my thinking was Alexis de Tocqueville's *Democracy in America*, especially as it pertains to the American penchant for association and the doctrine of "self-interest well understood." I recommend the English language edition published in 2000 featuring Harvey Mansfield's lengthy and luminous introduction.

Introduction

Page 1: Wendell Berry's quotation comes from the article "The Futility of Global Thinking," in the September 1989 issue of *Harper's Magazine*. It is an adaptation of Berry's commencement address to the College of the Atlantic, in Bar Harbor, Maine.

Chapter 1

Page 8: Section 68 of the Vermont Constitution reads: "a competent number of schools ought to be maintained in each town unless the general assembly permits other provisions for the convenient instruction of youth."

162

Page 8: For the development and current setup of Vermont's town tuitioning program, see Sternberg, Libby, "Lessons from Vermont," 2001 (http://www.cato.org/pubs/briefs/bp67.pdf)

Page 11: In an interview Louv explains that Nature-deficit disorder is "the cumulative effect of withdrawing nature from children's experiences, but not just individual children." Families, communities and cities experience it too. "Really, what I'm talking about is a disorder of society—and children are victimized by it." (http://dir.salon.com/story/mwt/feature/2005/06/02/Louv/print.html)

Page 12: Berry, "The Futility of Global Thinking," *Harper's Magazine* (September 1989).

Page 13: Carolyn Hoxby's "gold-standard" study of the effect of charter schools on student achievement in New York City can be accessed online at: (http://www.scribd.com/doc/20026658/How-NYC-Charter-Schools-Affect-Achievement-Sept2009)

Page 16: "A survey of state education agencies found that, in 2000-01, more than 4 million students with limited proficiency in English were enrolled in public schools across the nation, making up almost 10 percent of the total pre-K through 12th grade public school enrollment." Data retrieved from the EPE research center, URL: (http://www.edweek.org/rc/issues/english-language-learners/)

Page 18: High quality studies of vouchers generally show small but measurable improvement among participants. See the notes to chapter two for links to voucher studies and a discussion of them.

Page 19: For an overview of Virginia Gilder's experiment, see "Public School Benefits of Private School Vouchers" by Nina Shokraii Rees, URL: (http://www.hoover.org/publications/policyreview/3908721.html) and the September 29, 1997 *New York Times* story by James Dao.

Page 19: For more about single sex education, see the National Association for Single Sex Public Education (NASSPE) website. NASSPE Founder Leonard Sax wrote an excellent book on the subject titled *Why Gender Matters (2005)*. Information on changes to Title IX was taken from Sax's summer, 2002 article in *Women's Quarterly*.

Page 20: Test score results for BCCS are taken from the school's website: (http://www.brighterchoice.org)

Page 20-21: Visit the Ohio Department of Education website under "Scholarship Programs" for more details on the Cleveland voucher program. The U.S. Supreme Court case that ruled religious schools eligible to participate in the voucher program was the 2002 case, *Zelman v. Simmons-Harris*. The Court concluded that the Cleveland program offered "true private choice" and is "neutral in all respects toward religion." The decision can be accessed online at, URL: (http://www.law.umkc.edu/faculty/projects/ftrials/conlaw/zelman.html)

Page 21: Data on how unsafe some Cleveland public schools were came from "Blocking the Exits" by Clint Bolick in the May-June 1998 issue of the Hoover Institution journal *Policy Review*.

Page 22: Arizona State University reports that by the end of 2007, for-profit EMOs (Education Management Organizations) managed nearly 500 public schools in 31 states. These schools serve about 230,000 students, and over the last several years this number has remained stable. URL: (http://epsl.asu.edu/ceru/Documents/EPSL-0708-239-CERU .pdf)

Page 22: For more on the story of Chris Whittle and Edison Schools, see James Glassman's September 7, 2005 *Wall Street Journal* article, "An Entrepreneur Goes to School."

Page 23: For more discussion on the importance of family variables on student achievement v. other variables, see Caroline M. Hoxby, "If Families Matter Most, Where Do Schools Come In?" (Chapter 5 in the book *A Primer on America's Schools*) and available online at URL: (http://www.closingtheachievementgap.org/cs/ctag/view/resources/6)

Page 24: Indiana high school basketball and school vouchers were discussed by Michael Gerson in "The Hoops Factor," *U.S. News & World Report* (November 10, 1997), page 60.

Chapter 2

Page 27: NCES data puts the number of homeschooled students in the U.S. at over a million and rising. Homeschool advocates say the number is higher, up to well over two million. See Milton Gaithner's "Homeschooling Goes Mainstream," *Education Next* (Winter 2009) for a good overview.

Page 30: James Coleman's work on social capital was extensive. I borrow his definition of social capital from his 1990 work, *Foundations of Social Theory* (Cambridge, Harvard University Press), chapter 12.

Page 31: Studies of the academic performance of students in charter school show wide variance among schools. A 2009 study by Stanford's Center for Research on Education Outcomes (CREDO) states: "While the report recognized a robust national demand for more charter schools from parents and local communities, it found that 17 percent of charter schools reported academic gains that were significantly better than traditional public schools, while 37 percent of charter schools showed gains that were worse than their traditional public school counterparts, with 46 percent of charter schools demonstrating no significant difference."

Page 32: The Milwaukee Parental Choice Program reports 19,739 students in 125 voucher schools in January 2009. On his blog, University of Arkansas professor Jay P. Greene has compiled a list of high quality studies (including two of Milwaukee's program) of the effect of vouchers on participating students. Greene reports, "9 of the 10 analyses show significant, positive effects for at least some subgroups of students." URL: (http://jaypgreene.com/2008/08/21/voucher-effects-on-participants/)

Page 32: For more on the unorthodox coalition of Republican politicians, conservative foundations, and black parents for urban voucher programs, see James Ryan and Michael Heise, "The Political Economy of School Choice" *Yale Law Journal* (2002). In Milwaukee, the key players included Republican Governor Tommy Thompson; Michael Joyce, president of the conservative Milwaukee-based Lynde and Harry Bradley Foundation; Annette "Polly" Williams, a liberal African American state legislator, and Howard Fuller, the Milwaukee superintendent of schools. For more on this coalition, see Jim Carl, "Unusual Allies: Elite and Grass-roots Origins of Parental Choice in Milwaukee," *Teachers College Record* (Winter 1996).

Page 33: David Whitman's book, *Sweating the Small Stuff,* is available online in PDF format: URL: (http://www.edexcellence.net/detail/news.cfm?news_id=733&id=). The quote is found on page 260.

Page 34: The volunteer quoted is Dolores Herbstreith, a retired business owner who tutored students at Notre Dame Middle School for two years. It is taken from an article in the *Milwaukee Journal Sentinel* (June 5, 2008).

Page 35: Coleman's *Public and Private High Schools* found that Catholic schools had more social capital. In *Foundations of Social Theory* he described "primordial social structure" as "a normative structure which enforced obligations, guaranteed trustworthiness, induced efforts on behalf of others, and on behalf of the primordial corporate bodies themselves, and suppressed free riding. The social capital has been eroded, leaving many lacunas. Perhaps the most important area in which erosion has occurred is in the regeneration of society through the nurturing of the next generation..." (page 651).

Page 35: In June 2005, on the 15th anniversary of the voucher program, the *Milwaukee Journal Sentinel* published a 7-part series about the program. The quote is taken from the June 12, 2005 article by Allan Borsuk and Sarah Carr.

Page 36: Discussion of Milwaukee's voluntary busing program is adapted from James Ryan and Michael Heise, "The Political Economy of School Choice." URL: (http://papers.ssrn.com/abstract=292127)

Page 38: The number of students enrolled in online schools is taken from Donna Fuscaldo, "Online K-12 Schools Grow in Popularity," FOX-Business.com (September 3, 2008).

Page 39: Information on Adventist education was obtained from Seventh Day Adventist education websites. URLs: (http://www.nadeducation.org /intro & http://education.gc.adventist.org/)

Page 41: Quote on bowdlerized mainstream textbooks is taken from Diane Ravitch. "Education after the culture wars." *Dædalus* 131, no. 3 (Summer 2002). The article can be accessed online at URL: (http://www.catholiceducation.org/articles/education/ed0188.html). Ravitch also compiled a list of banned words in her March 2003 article in *The Atlantic*, "The Language Police." Examples include: Blind leading the blind (banned as handicapism), Busybody (banned as sexist, demeaning to older women), God (banned), Huts (banned as ethnocentric; replace with "small houses"), Jungle (banned; replace with "rain forest"), Old wives' tale (banned as sexist; replace with "folk wisdom"). The list is long and telling, and if you find it insane, consider your choice of words carefully: Insane (banned as offensive; replace with "person who has an emotional disorder or psychiatric illness").

Page 43: Information on one-room schoolhouses taken from Jodi Wilgoren, "The One-Room Schoolhouse," *New York Times* (August 6, 2000).

Page 44: Data on Montessori Schools in Washington State and Seattle taken from URL: (http://www.privateschoolreview.com/state_montessori_schools/type/10/stateid/WA) For more on the Montessori view that it is critically important for the youngest children to use concrete "hands-on" materials, see the article "Too Much Too Early," by Tufts professor David Elkind. He writes: "The natural world is the infant's and young child's first curriculum, and it can only be learned by direct interaction with things. Learning about the world of things, and their various properties, is a time-consuming and intense process that cannot be hurried. This view of early-childhood education has been echoed by all the giants of early-childhood development—Froebel, Maria Montessori, Rudolf Steiner, Jean Piaget, and Lev Vygotsky. It is supported by developmental theory." URL: (http://www.besthome-schooling.org/articles/david_elkind.html)

Page 45: Barbara Walters ABC-TV special, "The 10 Most Fascinating People of 2004."

Page 47: Mr. Arthur proudly showed me his own schools' achievement test results, URL: (http://www.arthuracademy.org/amazingresults.html) and pointed me towards research (Project Follow Through) indicating that Direct Instruction is effective in improving achievement test scores. URL: (http://darkwing.uoregon.edu/~adiep/ft/grossen.htm)

Chapter 3

Page 51: See Dorothy Sayers, "The Lost Tools of Learning." URL: (http://www.gbt.org/text/sayers.html)

Page 53: A *Casper Star-Tribune* poll found that 70 percent of people in Casper supported a neighborhood enrollment preference, while 50 percent of people polled supported the district's "schools of choice" policy. *Casper Star-Tribune* (October 21, 2008).

Page 56: The cost study for an "adequate" education in South Dakota can be found at URL: (http://www.sdallianceforeducation.org/object/u/AdequacyStudy.pdf). For the 2007-2008 school year, White Lake School District received $623,000 from local property tax contributions, $11,000 from the county, $550,000 from the state, and $144,000 from the federal government. The school is eligible for Title I federal funding because more than 50 percent of its students are from families below the poverty line. White Lake per pupil spending was $8,173. Quote from "Who could be against 'adequate' school funding," Erik Hanushek (February 9, 2004). URL: (http://www.hoover.org/pubaffairs/dailyreport/archive/2827251.html)

Page 59: Quote from URL: (http://www.maharishischoolsa.org/)

Page 60: Steve Diamond quoted his blog, URL: (http://globallabor.blogspot.com)

Page 61: "Schools in Chicago Are Called the Worst By Education Chief," *New York Times,* November 8, 1987.

Page 62: Abraham Lincoln, "Eulogy on Henry Clay," Springfield, Illinois, July 6, 1852. And "First Political Announcement," New Salem, Illinois, March 9, 1832.

Page 64: John Roberts opinion in *Meredith v. Jefferson County School Board* delivered June 28, 2007.

Pages 67-69: Joshua Dunn's book *Complex Justice* (University of North

Carolina Press, 2008) is an informative study of *Missouri v. Jenkins*. I quote from pages 3, 113, 123, 24, 129 and 98.

Page 68: Information gathered from a St. Louis Public Schools January, 2007 press release.

Page 70: Data on vocational and college prep education from "Is Vocational Education Still Necessary?" by Gray, Wang and Malizia, and "Trends among High School Seniors" from NCES. College dropout numbers come from "Diplomas and Dropouts" by Hess et al, URL: (http://www.aei.org/paper/100019)

Chapter 4

Page 72: PISA results from 2006 show the United States behind the average for OECD countries in both science and math. However, TIMSS scores from 2007 show math scores for both U.S. fourth-grade and eighth-grade students are slightly above the mean. URL: (http://nces.ed.gov/pubs2008/2008016_1.pdf)

Pages 73-75: "Busing's Boston Massacre" (*Policy Review,* December 1998) by Matthew Richer is an excellent overview of how racial busing disrupted Boston communities.

Page 73-74: Boston's Suffolk University has compiled dozens of fascinating interviews with people involved with or affected by Boston busing. The transcript of the interview with Lewis Finfer and the others can be accessed at URL: (http://www.suffolk.edu/archive/18020.html)

Page 74: Supreme Court Justice Clarence Thomas wrote in *Missouri v. Jenkins* (1995): "Brown I [One] did not say that "racially isolated" schools were inherently inferior; the harm that it identified was tied purely to de jure segregation, not de facto segregation." It announced "the simple, yet fundamental truth that the Government cannot discriminate among its citizens on the basis of race..."

Page 77: Test scores are taken from Pacific Rim website, URL: (http://www.pacrim.org/test_scores.htm)

Page 77: Data on charter school applications in Boston taken from URL: (http://charterschoolsboston.com/)

Page 77: Data on town wealth and per pupil spending by quintile taken from Connecticut Department of Education, URL: (http://www.sde.ct.gov/sde/lib/sde/PDF/dgm/report1/basiccon.pdf) and (http://www.sde.ct.gov/sde/LIB/sde/PDF/dgm/report1/cpse2005/table3.pdf).Test scores are taken from the 2005 NAEP, reported by ConnCan in "Policy Brief #1: The Achievement Gap."

Page 79: Per pupil expenditure figures as reported by school districts and states may be artificially low. Andrew Coulson, education analyst at the libertarian Cato Institute, found that in Washington DC "the spending figure cited most commonly is $8,322 per child, but total spending is close to $25,000 per child..." For more, see Coulson's "The Real Cost of Public Schools," *Washington Post,* April 6, 2008. This shouldn't matter when comparing spending in districts in Connecticut so long as underreporting is equally prevalent across districts.

Page 82: "They are stronger, younger and scarier" Star-Ledger (October 6, 2002).Page 85: *Wisconsin V. Yoder,* decided May 15, 1972. URL: (http://www.oyez.org/cases/1970-1979/1971/1971_70_110/)

Page 87: Adam Smith, *Theory of Moral Sentiments,* Pt.6, Sec.2, Ch.2.

Page 88: The 1997 report on Pennsylvania's Intermediate Units can be accessed at URL: (http://jsg.legis.state.pa.us/IUREPORT.PDF)

Page 89: *Marraro v. Commonwealth,* decided March 2, 1998. URL: (http://www.schoolfunding.info/states/pa/MARRERO.pdf)

Page 90: The consolidation proposal can be found on the Arkansas Policy Foundation website. URL: (http://www.reformarkansas.org/). Jay P. Greene's caution against consolidation comes from his July 2, 2008 article, "Consolidating school districts not always beneficial," *Arkansas Democrat Gazette.*

Pages 90-91: Two histories of school district consolidation are Andrew Coulson's "District Consolidation" (URL: http://www.mackinac.org/article.aspx?ID=8663) and William Fischel, *Making the Grade: The Economic Evolution of American School Districts* (University of Chicago Press, 2009).

Page 91: Quotes from Walter Isaacson's "How to Raise the Standard in America's Schools," *Time* (April 15, 2009); Louis Gerstner's "Lessons from 40 years of education 'reform,'" *Wall Street Journal* (December 1, 2008); Arne Duncan's speech to the Annual Meeting of the American Council on Education, February 9, 2009.

Chapter 5

Pages 94-95: See the Wake County Schools' Department of Growth and Planning website for more information on the current assignment plan. URL: (http://www.wcpss.net/)

Page 96: Take Wake Schools Back has the URL: (http://www.take-wakeschoolsback.com/) Wake Cares founder Kathleen Brennan wrote in the *Raleigh News and Observer* (February 6, 2009). The Children's Political Action Committee has the URL: (http://www.wakesca.org/). *The News and Observer* article comparing Raleigh and Charlotte schools is T Keung Hui, "Whose Schools Work Better?" (February 8, 2009).

Page 98: *Democracy in America,* translated and edited by Harvey Mansfield (2000), at Pt. IV, Ch. 6: "What kind of despotism democratic nations have to fear."

Page 99: The text of Senate Bill 10 can be found at URL: (http://www.legis.state.ga.us/legis/2007_08/pdf/sb10.pdf)

Page 100: The text of the statute establishing McKay scholarships can be found at URL: (http://www.floridaschoolchoice.org/information/mckay/)

Page 101: Kathleen Wylie's study "Can Vouchers Deliver Better Education" (1998) is at URL: (http://www.nzcer.org.nz/pdfs/5835.pdf)

Page 102: The Manhattan Institute studies of the McKay program are by Jay Greene and Greg Forster (2003) and Jay Greene and Marcus Winters (2008).

Page 103: Barnes and de Vice, "Court Weighs Funding for Special Education" *Washington Post,* April 27, 2009.

Page 103-104: *Forest Grove School District v. T.A,* decided June 22, 2009.

Page 105: The foundation in Mobile tracked high school students who should have graduated with the class of 2006, starting from their time in middle school until two years after they would have graduated: "From sixth grade, only 55.7 percent of the students graduated." The study found that boys are far more likely to drop out than girls. At the high school level, boys account for 59 percent of the dropouts. "The big challenge is to keep kids in school," *Press Register* (February 3, 2009).

Page 107: Paul Tough's "A Teachable Moment," *New York Times Sunday Magazine,* (August 14, 2008).

Page 110: Frederick Hess, "The New Stupid," January, 2009 at URL: (http://www.frederickhess.org/5136/the-new-stupid)

Page 113: Statistics on paddling in public schools come from URL: (http://www.corpun.com/counuss.htm)

Page 114: Peter Applebome, "Rancor where private school parents make public school decisions," *New York Times* (April 25, 2009).

Page 115: "Memphis' public school choice program gives parents options for selecting their children's school," by Nicole Ashby, *The Achiever* (October, 2005).

Page 116: Delta Prep student test scores are reported on the school's website, URL: (http://www.deltacollegeprep.org/results.htm)

Page 117: Cynthia Howell, "Charter school group gets $2.6 million grant," *Arkansas Democrat Gazette* (October 14, 2008).

Chapter 6

Page 122: The Texas statute creating the PEG program is at URL: (http://www.statutes.legis.state.tx.us/Docs/ED/htm/ED.29.htm)

Page 123: With vouchers, parents could hypothetically exercise direct rather than indirect control over their child's classmates—if schools were allowed to discriminate in accepting students based on socioeconomic status, cognitive ability etc. Parents worry that regulations will prohibit schools from doing this.

Page 123: See Joshua Benton, "Getting a Choice with Few Options," Dallas Morning News (February 4, 2002), on the lack of Texas student transfers.

Page 123: On CEO Foundation's Horizon Program see Peterson, Meyers, Howell "San Antonio voucher program serves working poor" (1999). URL: (http://www.hks.harvard.edu/news-events/news/press-releases/san-antonio-school-voucher-program-serves-working-poor,-study-finds). See also Frederick Hess, *Revolutions at the Margins: The Impact of Competition on Urban School Systems,* (Brookings Institution Press, 2002), pp. 179.

Page 128: In *Abington Township v. Schempp* (1963), the court ruled, "It certainly may be said that the Bible is worthy of study for its literary and historic qualities. Nothing we have said here indicates that such study of the Bible or of religion, when presented objectively as part of a secular program of education, may not be effected consistently with the First Amendment." And in *Epperson v. Arkansas* (1968), the "study of religions and of the Bible from a literary and historic viewpoint, presented objectively as part of a secular program of education, need not collide with the First Amendment's prohibition..."

Page 128: The article in *Time* is "The case for teaching the Bible," March 22, 2007.

Page 129: the Urban Institute, "The New Demography of America's

Schools," URL: (http://www.urban.org/UploadedPDF/311230_new_demography.pdf)

Page 129: Nathan Glazer, "Seasons Change," 7/19/06, URL: (http://educationnext.org/seasonschange/)

Page 129: E.D. Hirsch, *Cultural Literacy,* (Vintage edn. 1988) pages 18, 93.

Page 130: For more information on the Arizona Tax Credit, see the Arizona Department of Revenue website, URL: (http://www.azdor.gov/researchstats/schooltaxcredit.htm)

Page 131: The Arizona Supreme Court case that ruled the tax credit program constitutional is *Kotterman v. Killian.* The Arizona ACLU filed *Winn v. Garriot,* charging that the program's implementation is unconstitutional. A federal district court dismissed the lawsuit, but the 9th U.S. Circuit Court of Appeals overturned its ruling. The U.S. Supreme Court sustained the 9th's decision, so the case is back in district court.

Page 131-132: Adam Schaeffer, "The Public Education Tax Credit," *Cato Policy Analysis* #605, December 5, 2007 at URL: (http://www.cato.org/pub_display.php?pub_id=8812)

Page 133: John Taylor Gatto, "Beyond Money: Deschooling and a New Society," (1995) at URL: (http://www.swaraj.org/shikshantar/gatto differentteacher.html)

Page 134: George Will ably describes how knowledge increases economic returns on a July 24, 2008 Cato Institute podcast discussion of his book, *One Man's America.*

Page 134: For a discussion of Matthew Crawford's book, see my review in the *Washington Times* (August 2, 2009).

Page 135: For more on the implementation of Weighted Student Funding in Hawaii, see URL: (http://www.grassrootinstitute.org/GrassrootPerspective/LocalControl.shtml)

Page 136: Fordham's report can be found at URL: (http://www.ed excellence.net/fundthechild/)

Page 136: Lisa Snell, *Weighted Student Funding Yearbook,* (2009).

Page 136: The remarks about weighted student funding come from a PBS-sponsored debate on it. A transcript can be found at URL: (http://www.pbs.org/merrow/podcast/transcripts/52WeightedStudentDebate.pdf)

Page 137: University of New Hampshire professor Matthew Parks blogs at URL: (http://republican101.us/)

Page 137: Pacific Research Institute's study is "Not as Good as You Think," (September, 2007). URL: (http://www.pacificresearch.org/doc Lib/20070924_Middleclass.pdf)

Page 138: See Brunner, Sonstelie and Thayer, "Capitalization and the Voucher: An Analysis of Precinct Returns from California's Proposition 174," Journal of Urban Economics (November, 2001).

Page 138: William Fischel, "Why Voters Veto Vouchers: Public Schools and Community-Specific Social Capital," (2004). See page 12: "…voters in smaller districts disproportionately opposed the 1993 statewide voucher initiative." (Dartmouth Economics Working Paper, 2004). URL: (http://papers.ssrn.com/sol3/papers.cfm?abstract_id=306861)

Page 140: On minority support for vouchers, see Howell, Peterson, West, "What Americans think about their schools," *Education Next* (Fall, 2007).

Page 140: See Terry Moe, *Schools, Vouchers and the American Public* (Brookings Institution Press, 2002). Quote on page 217.

Page 141: See Phil Brand, "Unions Frantic," Human Events (October, 9, 2007) and George Will, "Utah's School Showdown," *Washington Post* (November 1, 2007).

Page 141: The National Education Association spent nearly $3.2 million on the campaign against vouchers, while Patrick Byrne and his family donated more than $2.7 million of the $3.8 million raised by the pro-voucher group, Parents for Choice in Education. Precinct data comes from URL: (http://www.uselectionatlas.org/RESULTS/datagraph.php?year=2007&fips=49&f=0&off=50&elect=0)

Page 141: Fischel, "Why Voters Veto Vouchers" (Dartmouth Economics Working Paper, 2004). URL: (http://papers.ssrn.com/sol3/papers.cfm?abstract_id=306861)

Page 143: Leah Barker, one of the lead spokesmen for Utah vouchers, quoted in "State Constitutionality and Adequacy: Signposts of Concern on Utah's Path Toward Developing Vouchers." By Ferrin, Ellis, Hallam, *Brigham Young University Law Review* (March 1, 2008).

Page 143, 145: George F. Will, "Where Paternalism Makes the Grade," *Washington Post* (August 21, 2008).

Chapter 7

Page 147: On elitism, I think Charles Murray says it best in his book *Real Education:* "I will spend no time on the argument that special treatment of the academically gifted is elitist. It has no moral standing. A special ability is a child's most precious asset. When it comes to athletic and musical ability, no one considers withholding training that could realize those gifts. It is just as senseless, and as ethically warped, to withhold training that can realize academic ability." (Page 147).

Page 148: Scott E. Carrell and Mark L. Hoekstra, "Domino Effect," *Education Next,* August, 19, 2009.

Page 149: The study of gifted education is Colangelo, Assouline and Gross, "A Nation Deceived: how schools hold back America's brightest students," (John Templeton Foundation, 2004).

Page 149: For information on how "proficiency" measures incentivize teachers and schools to focus on children near the proficiency "bubble," see Neil and Schanzenbach "Left Behind by Design: Proficiency Counts and Test-Based Accountability," (2007). URL: (http://www.aei.org/docLib/20070716_NealSchanzenbachPaper.pdf)

Page 150: Harvey Mansfield's Introduction to *Democracy in America* (2000), p. lxvii.

Page 153: John Taylor Gatto, "I quit I think," (1991) at URL: (http://www.johntaylorgatto.com/underground/prologue2.htm) and *Dumbing Us Down: The Hidden Curriculum of Compulsory Schooling,* (1992, 2nd edn. 2002).

Page154: Tony Woodlief, "Why Some Kids Aren't Heading to School Today," September, 2, 2008 at URL: (http://pajamasmedia.com/blog/why-some-kids-arent-heading-to-school-today/)

Page 155: Charles Murray, "The Happiness of the People," delivered March 11, 2009 at the American Enterprise Institute's Annual Dinner. Murray's remarks echo those of Russell Kirk, who observes in *The Conservative Mind* (1953): "Along with the consolations of faith, perhaps three other passionate human interests have provided the incentive to performance of duty—and the reason for believing that life is worth living—among ordinary men and women: the perpetuation of their own spiritual existence through the life and welfare of their children; the honest gratification of the acquisitive appetite through the accumulation and bequest of property; the comforting assurance that continuity is more probable than change—in other words, men's confidence that they participate in a natural and a moral order in which they count for more than flies of a summer." ("Flies of a summer" is Burke's phrase).

Page 156: Harvey Mansfield, Introduction to *Democracy in America* (2000), pages lxi, lxii and lxxv.

Page 157: Hess, Schneider, Carey, Kelly, "Diplomas and Dropouts: Which Colleges Actually Graduate Their Students (and Which Don't)" (AEI report, June 3, 2009).

Pages 158-159: Howell, Peterson, West, "What Americans think about their schools," *Education Next,* July 27, 2007.

Page 161: Edmund Burke, *Reflections on the Revolution in France:* "To be attached to the subdivision, to love the little platoon we belong to in society, is the first principle (the germ as it were) of public affections."

INDEX

Capital Research Center

Capital Research Center (CRC) was established in 1984 to support a healthy civil society, champion the American traditions of charity and philanthropy, and analyze developments in politics and public policy that pose dangers to the nonprofit sector.

Back issues of our three monthly newsletters Organization Trends, Foundation Watch and Labor Watch are available online at www.capitalresearch.org. Capital Research Center is supported by voluntary contributions. We accept no government grants or contracts.

We also publish the following books available directly from CRC [202/483-6900] or through the AmP Publishers Group [www.amppub-goup.com] or your bookseller:

Classical Education by Gene Edward Veith and Andrew Kern examines approaches to elementary and secondary schooling that tie the '3 Rs' to the moral and civic education of the Western tradition. (2001 rev. edn., 144 pp., $10)

The Great Philanthropists and the Problem of "Donor Intent" by Martin Morse Wooster contrasts philanthropic foundations that strayed from the intentions of their founders (e.g. Ford, Rockefeller, Pew) with others that honor their donors' intent. (2007 rev. edn., 272 pp., $14.95)

Should Foundations Live Forever? The Question of Perpetuity by Martin Morse Wooster considers government proposals and donor efforts to put limits on foundation life. (1998, 65 pp., $15)

Guide to Nonprofit Advocacy by James Dellinger. This handy reference profiles over 100 top public interest groups, liberal and conservative, that seek to influence law and public policy. (2008, 178 pp., $12)

The Green Wave: Environmentalism and its Consequences by Bonner Cohen exposes the inner workings of nonprofits and foundations that set the environmental agenda. (2006, 240 pp., $14.95)

Other CRC books include *Return to Charity: Philanthropy and the Welfare State; Global Greens: Inside the International Environmental Establishment; Guide to Feminist Organizations* and *Animal Rights: The Inhumane Crusade.*[Discounts available.]

For more information contact:

Capital Research Center
Terrence Scanlon, President
1513 16th Street, N.W.
Washington, DC 20036
202/483-6900
www.capitalresearch.org